W9-CSR-698

FUNDAMENTALS of TRADITIONAL MUSICAL NOTATION

OREGON

MAY 1 8 1987

STATE LIBRARY

FUNDAMENTALS of TRADITIONAL MUSICAL NOTATION

Albert C. Vinci

LIBRARY
EASTERN OREGON STATE COLLEGE
LA GRANDE, ORE. 97850
WITHDRAWN
FROM E.O.U. LIBRARY

THE KENT STATE UNIVERSITY PRESS

Copyright © 1985 by The Kent State University Press
All rights reserved.
Library of Congress Catalog Card Number 85-9754
ISBN 0-87338-319-2
Manufactured in the United States of America.

Library of Congress Cataloging in Publication Data
Vinci, Albert C.
  Fundamentals of traditional musical notation.

  Bibliography: p.
  1. Musical notation. I. Title.
MT35.V66 1985   781'.24   85-9754
ISBN 0-87338-319-2

To Susan and Alesandra for your patience

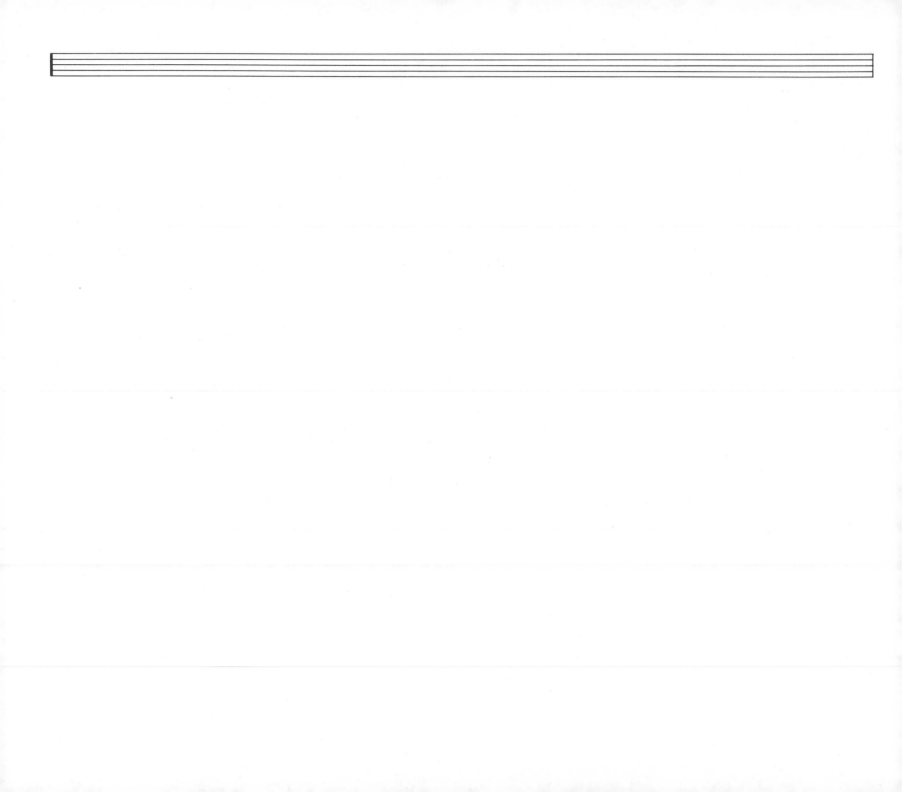

Contents

Preface and Acknowledgments

This book was compiled and written to serve as a practical ancillary reference for students of music enrolled in undergraduate music theory and related courses. Basic to the text is the concept that undergraduate music students can be guided and encouraged to develop and use a literate manuscript style applicable to the broadest range of music classes and performance.

Unlike other books on manuscript, notation, and the preparation of music, the student will not find exercises consisting of poor manuscript (contrived or facsimile) to be recopied, improved, or corrected. As in all phases of musical performance, the student must learn to create and recreate from a base of demonstrable training, discipline, and acquired knowledge. Notational practice should not differ from any other phase of learned musicianship in the training of professional musicians. Music theory and related courses remain fountainheads of materials to be recopied, improved, and corrected. After being made aware of the principles of notation presented in this reference, the student should then be held responsible and accountable for their implementation in all appropriate class work.

Every effort was made to avoid the inclusion of historical and developmental data relating to notation. The stylistic idiosyncrasies of notation employed by influential composers, arrangers, and publishing houses, while seemingly logical and innovative, often deviate from traditional norms and practice. The importance, validity, and uniqueness of these deviations and alternatives are not appropriate to the fundamental training of the undergraduate music student if such practices supplant the traditional concepts upon which they are based.

Traditional musical notation is a unique system of graphic symbols designed to embody musical thoughts and to communicate them to a performer. While notational symbols are confined to two-dimensional space, music flows in time, and such basic musical concepts as duration, pitch, volume, and timbre require adequately standardized graphic forms.

The two dimensions of the page or system of staves provide a grid system upon which musical time and pitch are graphically depicted. The left to right sequence of note and rest symbols expresses musical time, while the placement of noteheads in relation to staff lines and spaces represents the highness and lowness of pitch. The precise meaning of degrees of the staff is defined by clefs and accidentals, while the organization of time is designated by time signatures. Symbols that refer to dynamics, phrasing, articulation, and ancillary performance instructions enhance the musical thoughts depicted on the grid system. Of all the various dimensions of musical thought, only those of time and pitch are visually spatial. That these should be standardized into concise and uniform symbols is imperative for their communication.

An extensive and in-depth survey of notational practices represented by the current catalogues of reputable European, American, and Asian engraving and publishing firms (see Appendix) reveals a significant lack of uniformity regarding notational details within and among firms. This summary standardizes these notational ambiguities and forms a cohesive and viable base from which more complex notational developments may evolve.

The sequence of presentation represents a logical and functional approach which may be applicable to a wide range of theory curriculae. It does not represent those notational details and sequences employed by autographers, engravers, and copyists in the processes of publication. The standardizations formulated, though founded upon accepted engraving criteria and practices, are designed to accommodate manuscript notation and theoretical studies. This book is a summary of those fundamentals of traditional musical notation which form the core of literate musical communication.

Deep gratitude is expressed to Dr. Stanley Schleuter and Dr. Terry Kuhn for their suggestions, inspiration, and constant support throughout the course of this project; to Dr. W. Richard Shindle who nurtured and guided my interest in the historical developments of notational matters; and to Dr. James Waters whose advice, insights, patience, and persistence made the completion of this project possible.

1
The Staff
and Clefs

Example 1.1

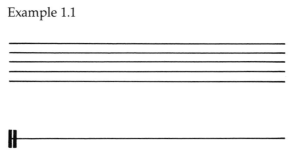

The staff, as a basic element of Western notation, may appear in a variety of forms, sizes, and uses, dependent upon the particular musical demand. The two most commonly employed staff forms, the five parallel lines with interformed spaces and the time continuum line (for use with percussion instruments of indefinite pitch), are illustrated in Example 1.1.

Serving as a grid system for notation, the staff forms provide meaning, reference, and definition to symbols placed upon them. It follows that a clear understanding of the staff and its various sizes is essential before approaching other aspects of traditional musical notation.

Since the advent of the printing press, engravers have derived and standardized nine size variants of the five-line staff. The vertical distance between the parallel lines of each staff variant is termed its rastral measurement and is identified by a rastral size number. Each rastral size staff is used for a specific genre of musical composition by publishing houses universally. The nine standardized rastral sizes of the five-line staff are shown in Example 1.2.

Example 1.2

Rastral no.	Staff	Trade names	Genre usage
0		Commercial or Public	Wire-bound manuscript books
1		Giant or English	Elementary band and orchestra works; instruction booklets
2		Regular, Common, or Ordinary	Sheet music, concertos, classics
3		Same as rastral size 2	Employed for works which contain a greater density of notational symbols
4		Peter	Folios, works for organ, etc.
5		Large middle	Band/wind ensemble music; sheet music
6		Small middle	Chorals; condensed sheet music
7		Cadenza	Pocket editions; cues in piano parts; military marches
8		Pearl	Thematic advertisement; ossia clarifications

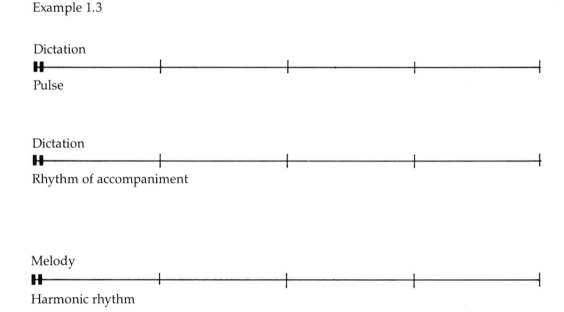

Example 1.3

Dictation

Pulse

Dictation

Rhythm of accompaniment

Melody

Harmonic rhythm

Musical genre, notational complexity, performance needs, and reproduction requirements are the primary considerations in the selection of staff forms for use with theory exercises. The majority of theory exercises can be provided for by the format of an 8½-by-11-inch page.

Both the time continuum line and modern five-line staves may be effectively used in theory pedagogy. The time continuum line staff may be used for the dictation and notation of rhythmic exercises. The single-line aspect of this staff allows for concentration on the metric and rhythmic details by visually removing the tonal implications that may be present with the use of the five-line staff. While the length of this staff is governed by the width of the page, the single-line aspect will permit a far greater number of staves per page than the five-line staff. Example 1.3 illustrates how the time continuum line staff may be used for the notation of rhythmic dictation.

The five-line staff may be used for all tonal exercises including melodic and harmonic examples that do not require a Grand Staff or multiple-stave systems. The most practical rastral size for the single five-line staff should be determined by the ease of comparative analysis, density of melodic and harmonic factors, minimum physical movement during notation, and maximum grading area. Rastral size 0 accommodates harmonic exercises easily with both open and closed noteheads, while rastral size 2 is ideal for melodic and scale exercises. Rastral size 0, if used for melodic exercises, would require noteheads much too large to gain speed of notation, and rastral size 2, in harmonic exercises, would make noteheads too close together for clear identification. A compromise of employing rastral size 1 would standardize the selection and mean a minimum of adjustment for both melodic and harmonic exercises.

The Grand Staff, used for keyboard notation, is the most prevalent staff form employed for theory exercises. When Chorale Style theory exercises require each staff of the Keyboard Grand Staff to become shared staves, that is, separately stemmed soprano and alto voices sharing the top staff, while the tenor and bass voices share the bottom staff, the distance between the staves proves to be far too restrictive. The restriction becomes apparent when one observes that the shared staff notation of the alto and tenor parts with downward and upward stems, respectively, causes cluttered visual space between the staves. To maintain correct visual perspective and notational ease, the distance between the staves may be increased through the use of the Chorale Grand Staff. The visual difference between the Keyboard Grand Staff and the Chorale Grand Staff is illustrated in Example 1.4.

Example 1.4

Keyboard Grand Staff

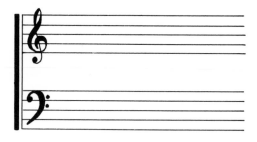

Chorale Grand Staff (shared staff)

Example 1.5

Grouping of two or more staves forms a staff system. Such systems can be very useful for purposes of clarification and illustration and offer the opportunity of visually restricting the information to the point under discussion. System formulation is accomplished with the use of the notational characters called the left-end bar line and the beam brace. The left-end bar line vertically connects the number of staves forming the system, while the beam brace may be used to delineate internal groupings of staves or unify all staves into one multiple-stave system. Example 1.5 shows the uses of the left-end bar line and beam brace in the formulation of multiple-stave systems which may be used to serve theory exercise needs.

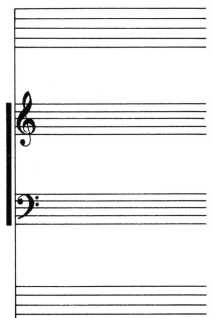

Continued on next page

Example 1.5 (*continued*)

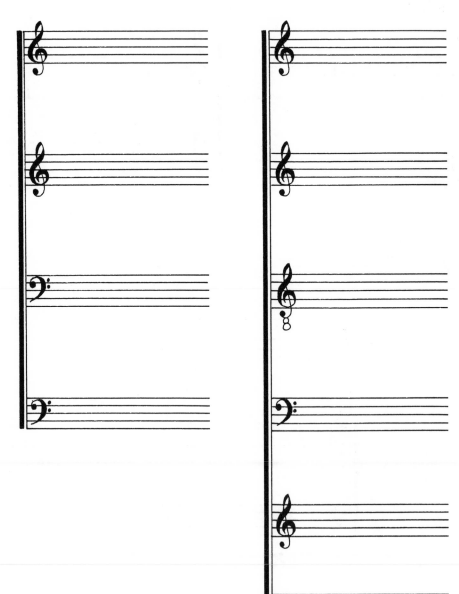

In modern notational practice, clefs are used to designate definite or indefinite pitches. The G, F, C (alto), and C (tenor) clefs designate definite pitches respectively. The percussion clef designates indefinite pitch and is used by instruments of indefinite pitch. It is also employed in a variety of settings beyond percussion notation, as shown later in Example 1.11.

In relating a specific pitch to a degree of the staff, the clef becomes the point of reference from which all other pitches are derived. The F clef (𝄢) designates the pitch F, and its placement and appropriate sizing require the following criteria: 1) the two vertical dots must be centered mid-space, respectively, above and below the fourth line of the staff, and 2) the 𝄢 portion must be proportional to the rastral size of the staff. Example 1.6 illustrates the correct notation of the F clef on the staff. Engraved clefs are included in Examples 1.6, 1.7, and 1.8 for comparative purposes.

Example 1.6

F    Engraved clef

Current use of the C clef (𝄡) is restricted to the two previously mentioned forms, commonly called the alto and tenor clefs. The centering of the visual focal point, as illustrated in Example 1.7, is essential to the designation of middle C.

Example 1.7

Engraved clefs

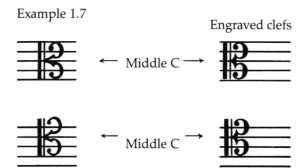

← Middle C →

← Middle C →

Because the accepted design of this clef is difficult to execute in manuscript notation, a variety of alternate designs have been substituted by composers and arrangers. The most commonly found alternative designs of the C clef, shown in Example 1.8, are not universally accepted and should be avoided.

Example 1.8

The G clef ( ) , the most frequently employed of the clefs, designates G on the second line of the staff. The line used to draw the clef sign must encircle the G line between the first and center lines of the staff and cross itself on the fourth line of the staff after forming a loop which extends approximately a third above the staff. Its downward path from the fourth line crossing should intersect the center of the encirclement, and it should terminate approximately a third below the staff with a slight left curl. (See Example 1.9.)

Example 1.9

Engraved clef

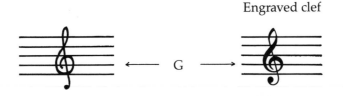

Example 1.10

The interrelatedness of definite pitch clefs may be best shown by placing them respectively on a Grand Staff, as in Example 1.10.

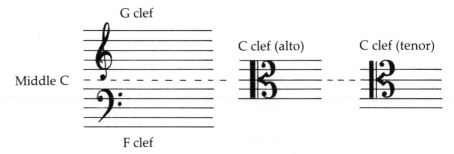

G clef

C clef (alto)   C clef (tenor)

Middle C

F clef

The percussion clef (**▮▮**) may be applied in numerous settings because it does not refer to definite pitch. Three of the most commonly applied placements are illustrated in Example 1.11.

Example 1.11

Cymbals   Drums

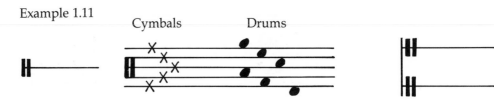

Example 1.12

First staff

Subsequent staves

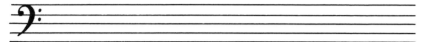

In traditional notational practice, the clef must be placed at the beginning of each staff throughout the composition. On single-stave systems (Example 1.12), it is not preceded by a left-end bar line.

Example 1.13

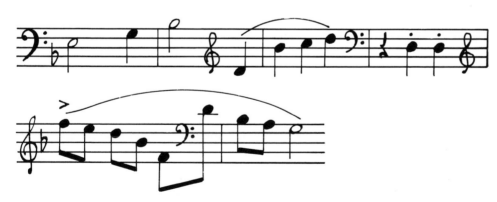

When a clef is changed during the course of a work, the new clef may appear anywhere within the measure of change. If the clef change affects the beginning of a measure in the middle of a staff, the new clef must be placed immediately before the bar line of that measure. If the first measure of a staff is affected by a clef change, the change of clef must be placed immediately before the final bar line of the preceding staff. Further, with the exception of the percussion clef which remains constant in size, the clef change should be approximately two-thirds normal size. Normal clef size is resumed at the beginning of the subsequent staff. Correct sizing and placement of changes of clef are illustrated in Example 1.13.

Leger lines placed above or below the five-line staff serve as temporary extensions of that staff. The rastral size of the staff must be reflected in the placement of the leger lines. Each leger line should extend beyond either side of a notehead approximately half the width of the notehead. Example 1.14 illustrates the placement and notehead use of normal length leger lines and noteheads.

Example 1.14

When both notes of an interval of a second require the use of one or more leger lines (Example 1.15), all leger lines between the staff and the second must be double length.

Example 1.15

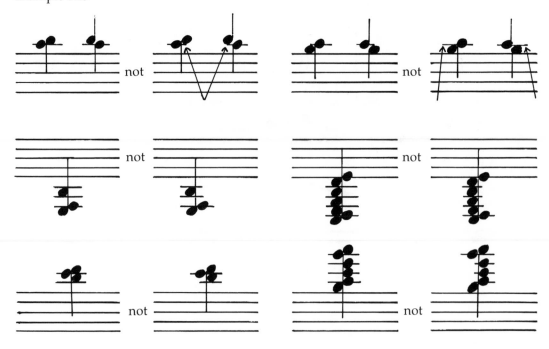

2
Symbols of Sound and Silence

Modern mensural notational practice consists of contrived notational symbols, each of which represents a single level of a sequence of fixed arithmetical relationships of time values. The symbols have been contrived in pairs and share similar descriptive names. Each pair consists of a symbol for sound and its measured duration called a note, while a symbol for silence and its measured duration is called a rest. Each note or rest symbol derives its name from its arithmetical relationship to the mensural level represented by the whole note and is equal in value to two of the next smaller level of time value. The modern mensuration levels, names, and pairs of symbols are illustrated in Example 2.1.

Example 2.1

Level	Durational Value	Names
1	Double value of level 2. No time signature designation numeral exists	Double whole note / Double whole rest
2	Basic level TSDN (time signature designation number): "1"	Whole note / Whole rest
3	Half the value of level 2 TSDN: "2"	Half note / Half rest
4	Half the value of level 3 TSDN: "4"	Quarter note / Quarter rest
5	Half the value of level 4 TSDN: "8"	Eighth note / Eighth rest
6	Half the value of level 5 TSDN: "16"	Sixteenth note / Sixteenth rest
7	Half the value of level 6 TSDN: "32"	Thirty-second note / Thirty-second rest
8	Half the value of level 7 TDSN: "64"	Sixty-fourth note / Sixty-fourth rest
9	Half the value of level 8 TSDN: "128"	One hundred and twenty-eighth note / One hundred and twenty-eighth rest

Traditional notational practice requires all mensural level noteheads to be elliptical. The distinctive internal shading of unstemmed and stemmed white noteheads (o 𝄽) continues in engraving practice, but modern notators have found it to be essentially cosmetic. While stem direction has generally been standardized in traditional notational practice, three different stem lengths continue to be employed by reputable engravers and publishers. These and their nomenclatures are illustrated in Example 2.1A. The stem length of a seventh has been selected for use throughout this summary.

Example 2.1A

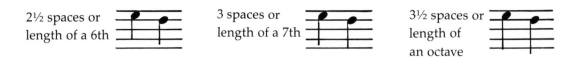

2½ spaces or length of a 6th   3 spaces or length of a 7th   3½ spaces or length of an octave

Graphic elements which combine to form the note symbols are structural additives with the exception that the first graphic elements are removed from the double whole note to form the subsequent whole note. (See Example 2.2.)

Example 2.2

Double whole note   to   Whole note

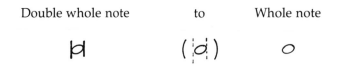

The formulation of the half note begins the sequential application of graphic elements as additives by attaching a vertical stem to one of the two sides of the elliptical whole note notehead. Downward stems are attached to the left side, and upward stems are attached to the right side. Example 2.3 illustrates the stem additive in the formulation of the half note, and Example 2.4 shows that the additive in the formulation of the quarter note is the closing of the elliptical half note notehead.

Example 2.3

Example 2.4

Example 2.5

Open flag position   Closed flag position

The flag, as the additive forming the eighth note, is one of the most difficult elements to draw accurately. Beginning as an addition to the stem-end, it returns by obliquely curving away from the stem, increasing its distance from the stem until the width of a notehead is reached. At this point, it turns inward to terminate half a notehead width from the stem approximately three-fourths the stem length. The flag is always to the right of the stem, creating what may be called "closed flag position" on downward stems, and "open flag position" on upward stems. The eighth note with open and closed flag positions are illustrated in Example 2.5.

Example 2.6

The formulation of the sixteenth note does not differ from that of the eighth note except with the precise placement of the second flag. It is placed between the first flag and the notehead approximately the width of half a staff-space away from the first flag. While the curvature of the first flag is paralleled by the second flag, its termination point is not exceeded. See Example 2.6 for the correct placement of the sixteenth note flag in open and closed flag position.

The consecutive flag additives which form the thirty-second, sixty-fourth, and one hundred and twenty-eighth notes significantly differ from previous flag placement only in that their addition to the stem extends its length, since they are positioned beyond the eighth note flag. Example 2.7 illustrates the correct placement of each of the above flags.

Noteheads and flags remain constant in size during formation of note symbols and do not diminish proportionally in size as time values diminish. The stem is the only additive that does not remain constant in that it must be lengthened to accommodate the increase in the number of flags attached to it.

All flagged notes may be grouped visually through the use of beams attached to stems in the same order and placement as flags as in Example 2.8. Specifics of mensural grouping and beaming practice are discussed in chapters 3 and 4 respectively.

Example 2.7

Normal stem length ⟶

⟶ Sixteenth-note flag
⟶ Eighth-note flag
⟶ Thirty-second-note flag
⟶ Sixty-fourth-note flag
⟶ One hundred and twenty-eighth note flag

Example 2.8

= Eighth notes

= Sixteenth notes

= Thirty-second notes

= Sixty-fourth notes

= One hundred and twenty-eighth notes

Example 2.9

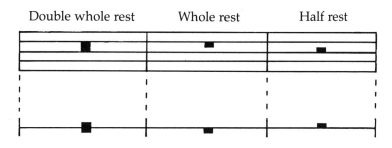

Double whole rest   Whole rest   Half rest

Rest symbols are not contrived from one cohesive structural scheme of additives. Rest symbols that are paired with the double whole, whole, and half notes are called beam rests and are illustrated in Example 2.9. As shown here, beam rests, in normal use, are placed in the third space of the five-line staff. All are of equal length, with the whole and half rests extending to mid-space, downward and upward respectively.

Example 2.10

Engraved quarter rest   Manuscript quarter rest   Common versions to be avoided

Because the quarter rest is structurally unrelated to all other rest symbols and probably the most difficult symbol to draw, it is the most subject to error. For this reason, Example 2.10 illustrates an engraved sample, a universally accepted manuscript sample, and a variety of commonly found versions which must be avoided.

Flagged rest symbols, paired to flagged notes, consist of identical additives. The basic flag rest consists of an obliquely slanting stem with a hook attached to the upper stem-end facing left. The hook should terminate with an attached dot placed mid-space. The placement of additional flag rests is governed by a sequence that differs from that employed in the addition of flags to flagged noteheads. On the five-line staff, the first (eighth rest) flag rest is centered between the second and fourth lines. Subsequent flag additions follow an alternating pattern of placement, with the exception of the one hundred and twenty-eighth rest flag which is traditionally placed between the first staff line and an implied first leger line below the staff. All flagged rests placed with the time continuum line staff are positioned above and/or below the line at identically spaced intervals. Example 2.11 illustrates placement of flag rests on the five-line and time continuum line staves.

Example 2.11

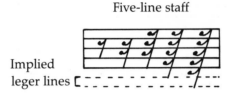

Five-line staff

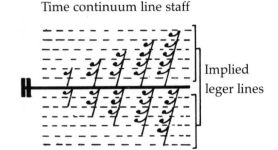

Time continuum line staff

Implied leger lines

Example 2.12

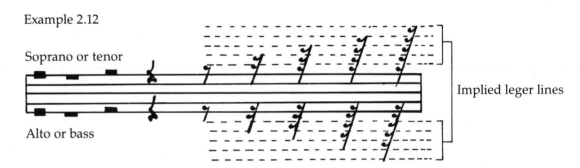

Soprano or tenor

Alto or bass

Implied leger lines

The repositioning of all rest symbols is necessary when they are present on a shared staff, as in Example 2.12. However, duplication of rest symbols between voices sharing a staff may be avoided when both voices have the same rhythm, through the use of normal rest placement. Example 2.13 illustrates normal rest placement with homophonic voices on a shared staff.

Example 2.13

in lieu of:

Example 2.14

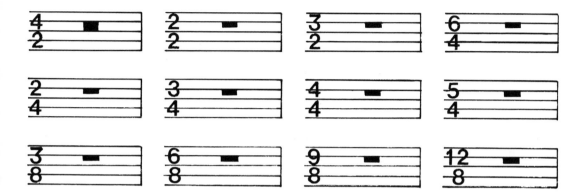

The whole rest is used to indicate a full measure rest in all time signatures with the exception of $\frac{4}{2}$, which requires a double whole rest. The placement of the whole rest is always immediately left of the arithmetical center of the measure, as shown in Example 2.14.

Example 2.15

On a shared staff, upper-part whole rests hang from the top line, while those of the lower part hang from the bottom line. Both upper- and lower-part whole rests may be placed hanging from a leger line outside the staff when normal placement interferes with notation. Example 2.15 illustrates these practices.

Example 2.16

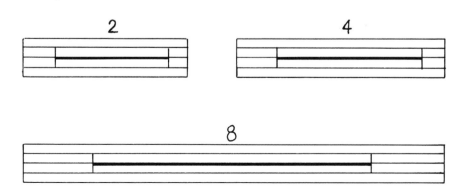

Two or more measures of rest may be indicated by a horizontal beam which straddles the center line of the staff and is the thickness of half a staff-space (Example 2.16). The length of the beam should be the center three-fourths of the measure. Each end of the beam is terminated with a short bar line drawn between the second and fourth lines of the staff, while the number of rest measures is indicated with an appropriate numeral centered between the two short bar lines a third above the staff.

All rest symbols, with the exception of the whole rest, are rhythmically spaced within measures similarly to notes. There are some basic principles governing the use of rests, most of which are concerned with the clarification of beats. Example 2.17 illustrates that in binary time signatures, such as $\frac{2}{4}$ and $\frac{4}{4}$, rests must not cross the middle of measures. Furthermore, dotted quarter rests in $\frac{2}{4}$ and $\frac{4}{4}$, and dotted eighth rests in $\frac{2}{8}$ and $\frac{4}{8}$, both shown in Example 2.18, may not be used on the first beat of the measure or across the middle of the measure.

Example 2.17

Example 2.18

Example 2.19

Correct

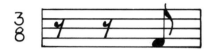

Incorrect

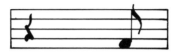

Example 2.20

Correct

Incorrect

In ternary time signatures such as $\frac{3}{4}$ and $\frac{3}{8}$ (Example 2.19), each beat must have its own rest, and two-beat rests are not employed. While a dotted quarter rest may used on the second beat of $\frac{3}{4}$ measures (Example 2.20), it may not be used on the first beat.

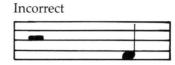

Example 2.21 illustrates that in $\frac{2}{8}$, $\frac{3}{4}$, and $\frac{4}{4}$, dotted quarter rests may not be placed after an eighth note which occurs on a beat.

Example 2.21

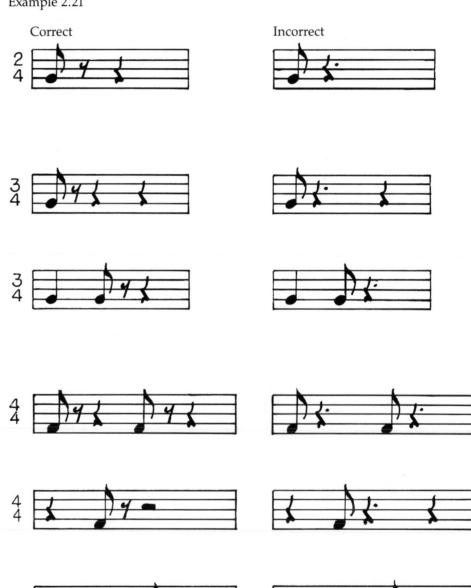

Example 2.22

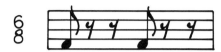 

Dotted quarter rests may be used for beat divisions normally beamed together in compound time signatures such as $\frac{6}{8}$, $\frac{9}{8}$, and $\frac{12}{8}$, and undotted quarter rests may only be used for the first two-thirds of such divisions (Example 2.22).

LIBRARY
EASTERN OREGON STATE COLLEGE
LA GRANDE. ORE. 97850

Undotted and dotted half rests are not used in the compound time signatures of $\frac{6}{8}$ and $\frac{9}{8}$ (Example 2.23). While the undotted half rest may also not be used in the compound time signature of $\frac{12}{8}$, a dotted half rest may indicate a half measure rest (Example 2.24). As in previous practice, the middle of the measure must remain clear.

Example 2.23

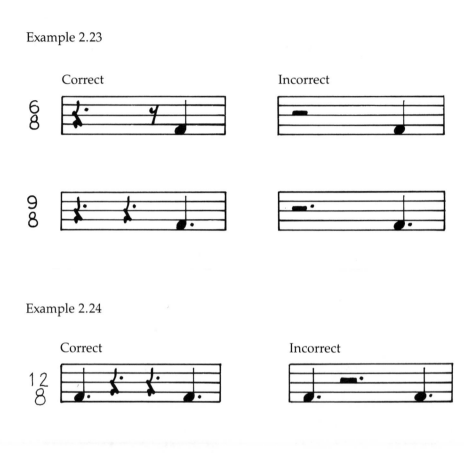

Example 2.24

Correct   Incorrect

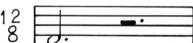

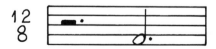

Example 2.25

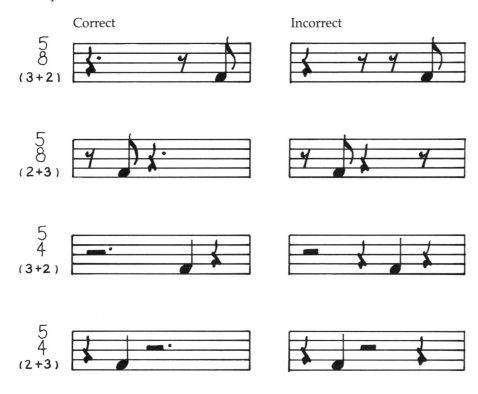

Correct   Incorrect

$\frac{5}{8}$
(3+2)

$\frac{5}{8}$
(2+3)

$\frac{5}{4}$
(3+2)

$\frac{5}{4}$
(2+3)

In such composite time signatures as $\frac{5}{8}$ and $\frac{5}{4}$, shown in Example 2.25, previously discussed practices apply only to the extent that the rests should reflect the rhythmic divisions within the measure.

Example 2.26

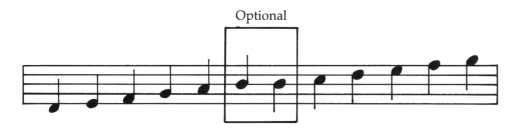

Optional

The determination of stem direction in traditional notational practice is based upon the placement of a notehead in relationship to the center line of the five-line staff. If the notehead is placed below the center line, the stem is attached to the right side of the notehead and extends vertically upward, while noteheads placed above the center line have stems attached to the left of the notehead extending downward. These practices are illustrated in Example 2.26.

Noteheads placed on the center line may have either upward or downward stem direction, a choice of direction usually determined by the individual notational context in which the notehead is employed. In most circumstances, a downward stem is preferred.

Noteheads placed above and below the staff through the use of leger lines have stems whose length must be extended to the center line of the staff, as in Example 2.27.

Example 2.27

Stems applied to unbeamed intervals and chords should be of normal length measured from the notehead nearest the stem-end. Unbeamed intervals and chords have stem direction determined by the notehead farthest from the center line of the staff. In Example 2.28, noteheads which determine stem direction are indicated by an asterisk, while Example 2.29 illustrates that intervals and chords whose noteheads are equally spaced from the center line have a preferred downward stem direction.

Example 2.28

Implied leger lines

Example 2.29

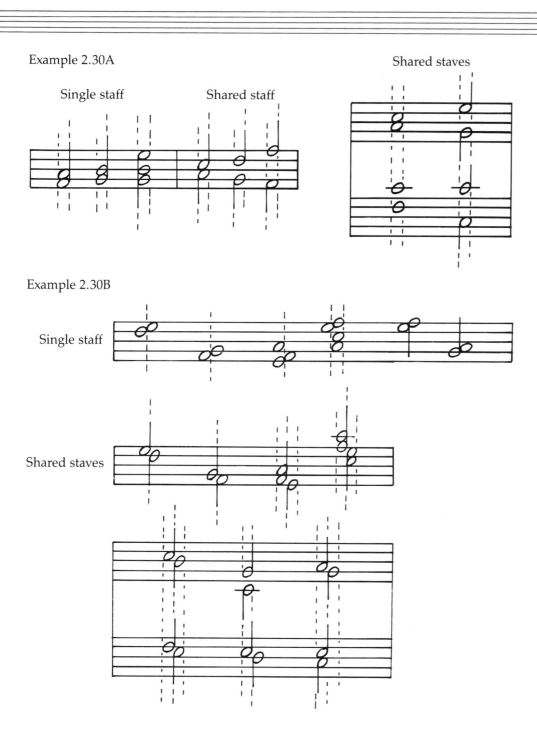

Example 2.30A

Single staff   Shared staff

Shared staves

Example 2.30B

Single staff

Shared staves

The vertical alignment of intervals or chords containing two or more noteheads placed on single or multiple staves may be symmetrical or asymmetrical. Noteheads placed vertically in line-to-line, space-to-space, and other more widely spaced arrangements are symmetrically aligned, while vertical notehead arrangements which contain seconds, that is, line-to-adjacent space or space-to-adjacent line, are asymmetrically aligned. Alignment of noteheads of a second requires the lower notehead to be placed left of the stem or implied stem placement with the exception of the shared staff. Seconds which occur between voices sharing a staff must be placed with the lower notehead to the right and the upper notehead to the left of stem or implied stem placement. Example 2.30A illustrates symmetrical alignment of vertical noteheads on single and shared staves, and Example 2.30B illustrates asymmetrical alignment of vertical noteheads with seconds on single and shared staves.

The occasional crossing of parts between two voices sharing a staff may require abnormal vertical alignment of noteheads. Equal note values between the voices require the lower voice notehead to be placed slightly left of the upper voice notehead to ensure that stems only touch the appropriate noteheads, as shown in Example 2.31A. Unequal note values between the voices require the notehead of greater value to be placed slightly right of the notehead of lesser value, as in Example 2.31B.

Example 2.31A

Example 2.31B

3
Beat and
Measure
Organization

Example 3.1A

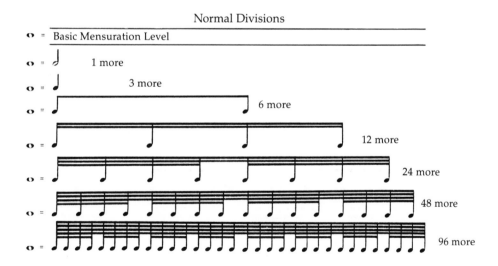

Normal Divisions

𝐨 = Basic Mensuration Level

𝐨 = ♩ 1 more

𝐨 = ♩ 3 more

𝐨 = 6 more

𝐨 = 12 more

𝐨 = 24 more

𝐨 = 48 more

𝐨 = 96 more

In traditional notational practice, the visual organization of note and rest symbols is governed by the arithmetical relationships between the mensural levels they represent. Mensural levels are normal divisions, by halves, quarters, eighths, and so on, of the basic mensuration level represented by the whole note. Each mensural level division may also be abnormally divided into thirds, fifths, sixths, sevenths, and so on. It is understood that, as a mensural level division is divided into smaller parts, the time value of the representative note also decreases. Example 3.1A illustrates that the mensuration level of the whole note serves as the basic level to which all other mensural level divisions refer.

Example 3.1B illustrates the abnormal divisions, correctly notated with appropriate grouping, bracketing, and/or beaming, contained within each of the mensural level divisions to the thirty-second note level.

Example 3.1B

Continued on next page

Example 3.1B (*continued*)

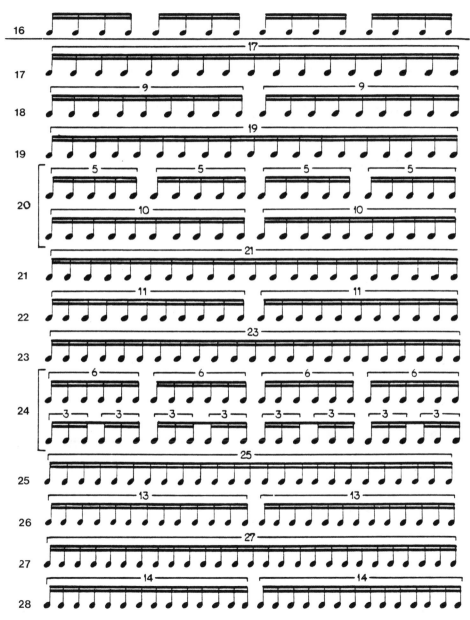

Continued on next page

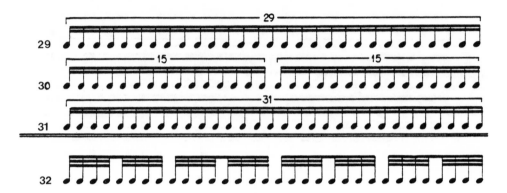

Example 3.1B (*continued*)

The abnormal divisions illustrated in Example 3.1B, consisting of triplets, quintuplets, sextuplets, and so on, are designated by brackets, numbers, and beams. To avoid confusion with slurs, brackets should be employed in lieu of the slur-like arc, and only combined with numbers if beams are broken or have been replaced with individually flagged notes. In such instances, the bracket must enclose the entire physical and visual space normally accorded the division, including such implied space for notes and rests represented by a composite note or rest symbol. Because articulation signs and slurs are normally placed opposite stems (or implied stems for unstemmed noteheads), brackets and numbers should be placed at stem-ends for unbeamed notes and aligned with beams for beamed notes to avoid interference with the placement of such signs. Unbracketed or bracketed numbers should be centered over or under the arithmetical middle of the abnormal division if a note or rest occurs at that point, or the visual middle if no note or rest symbol begins at that point. Unbeamed notes require the use of a bracketed number in all instances. Example 3.2 illustrates correct use and placement of bracketed and unbracketed numbers.

Example 3.2

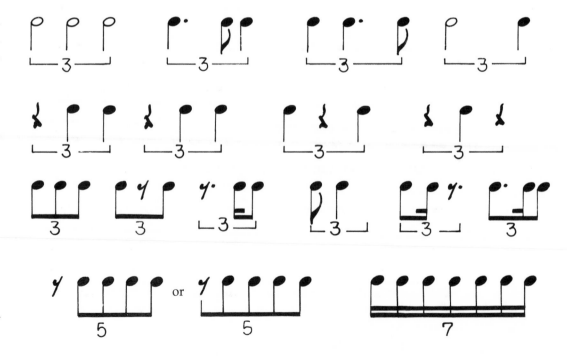

Example 3.3

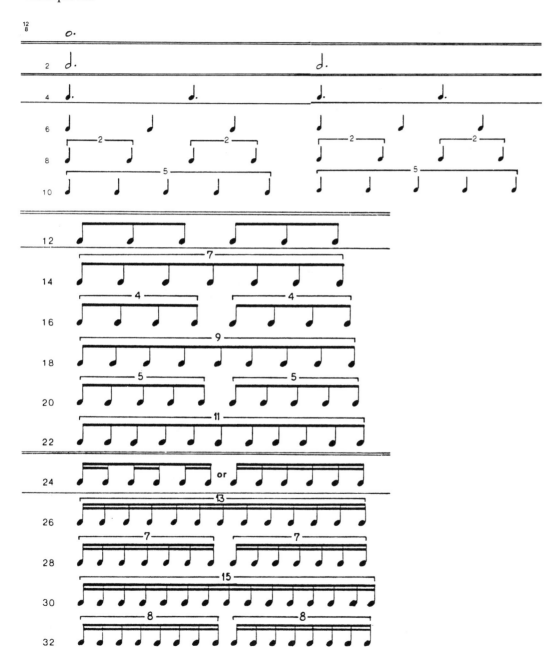

All previously discussed and illustrated examples of normal divisions have been based on undotted or binary note symbols, in which ternary divisions are considered abnormal. Dotted notes serving as normal divisions are divided normally into thirds, and binary divisions are considered abnormal. Unbracketed and bracketed binary numbers are used for abnormal divisions of dotted (ternary) note divisions. See Example 3.3.

Example 3.3 (*continued*)

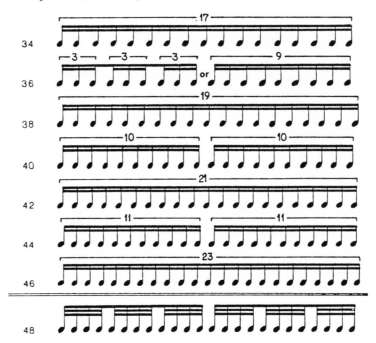

Two alternate methods of notating binary divisions within ternary mensural levels continue to be practiced in traditional notation. In the first method, the bracketed binary division is replaced with two dotted notes of the next smaller mensural level, thereby maintaining the arithmetical relationship between the mensural levels. Example 3.3A illustrates this practice.

Example 3.3A

Recommended practice
(Example 3.3)

Equally valid practice

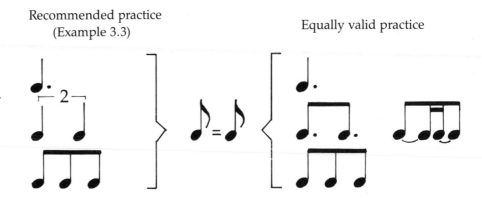

Example 3.3B

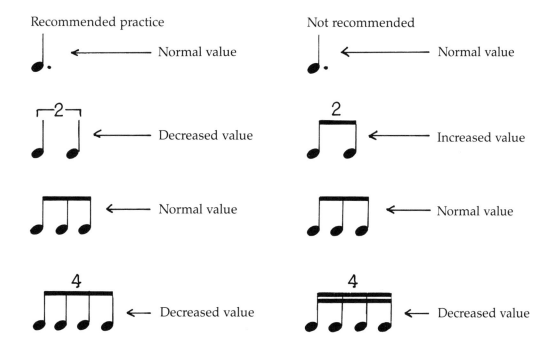

Recommended practice   Not recommended

Normal value

Normal value

Decreased value

Increased value

Normal value

Normal value

Decreased value

Decreased value

In the second method, two undotted notes of the next smaller mensural level replace the larger note symbols, but the number is maintained. This practice introduces the smaller note value symbol before its normal arithmetical relationship is appropriate (for example, three eighth notes equaling one dotted quarter note), and creates confusion in that these replacement notes are of longer duration than normally accorded them. This practice, illustrated in Example 3.3B, is not recommended.

The retention of note values of a regular note division until the next shorter note division is metrically appropriate remains in general use in traditional notational practice. Basic to this general use is the fact that its logical tenet of subdivision is applicable uniformly throughout all note divisions. Irregular note groupings, such as quintuplets, septuplets, and octuplets, should adhere to this practice.

Some influential contemporary composers have implemented the substitution of the shorter note values of the next smaller note division for these irregular note groupings, particularly at the sixteenth and thirty-second note-value levels. While this compromise practice may be defensible from the point of view that the irregular note groupings are closer in proximity to the next smaller note division than visually discernible in traditional practice, the concept does create a metrically illogical anomaly. Further, the substitution is not applied uniformly throughout all note divisions, and, most importantly, is not accepted into general practice.

I am convinced that an undergraduate music student should have a thorough grounding in the basic logic of traditional notational practice before being permitted to deviate from that practice in the solving of idiosyncratic problems. For these reasons, the compromise practice is not recommended.

Example 3.3C illustrates quintuplets, septuplets, and octuplets in traditional and compromise practices.

Example 3.3C

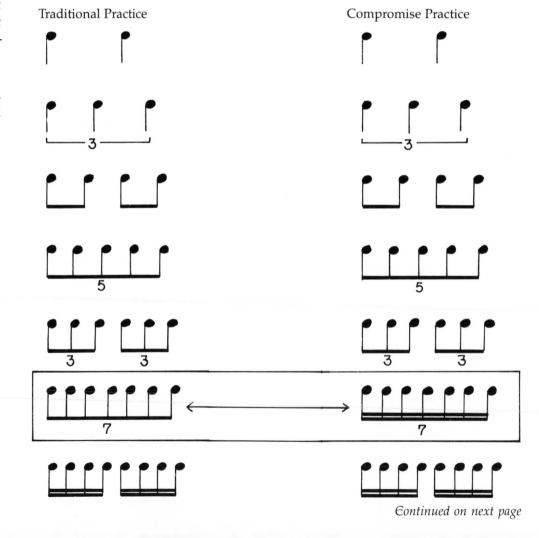

Continued on next page

Example 3.3C (*continued*)

Traditional Practice   Compromise Practice

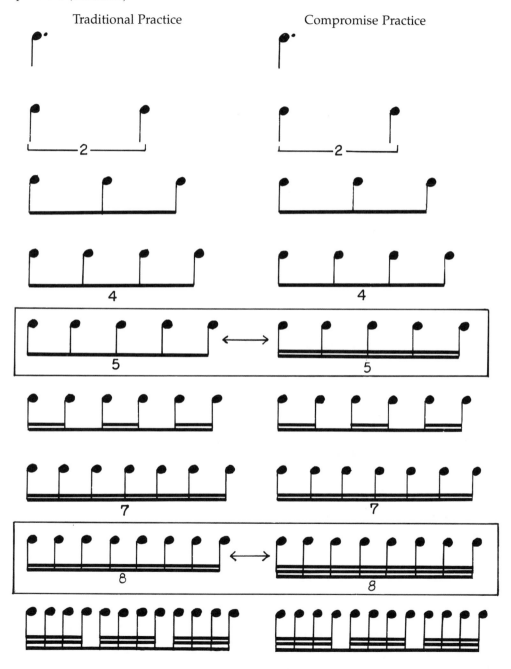

Notation within all measures, regardless of prevailing time signature, must visually divide each measure into proportional beats. Generally speaking, the spacing of noteheads and rests within any measure should be based upon arithmetical values and relationships of the symbols present in order to assist the performer's grasp of the rhythmic structure by visual means. Example 3.4 illustrates correctly and incorrectly proportioned beats within $\frac{2}{4}$, $\frac{3}{4}$, $\frac{4}{4}$, and $\frac{6}{8}$ measures containing combinations of rests and notes from normal and abnormal divisions.

Example 3.4

Example 3.5

Example 3.5 shows how notation must delineate beats and divisions within beats.

Measures which may be divided into equal halves normally, such as $\frac{4}{4}$ and $\frac{4}{8}$ measures, may have pairs of beats beamed together if each pair consists of equal length eighth notes, simple or identical rhythms. Example 3.6 illustrates that in either case, the middle of the measure must be clearly defined by the notation.

Example 3.6

Example 3.7

not

Similarly, notes or rests whose values cross the center of the measure must be broken into tied notes or two rests to permit visual identification of the middle of the measure as shown in Example 3.7.

Example 3.8

Dotted note   Equivalent value in tied notes

The basic value of note and rest symbols may be increased through the use of augmentation dots. Augmentation dots are always placed to the right of noteheads and rests in horizontal alignment at half staff-space distances. In Example 3.8, the basic value of a note (or rest) is increased by one-half with the use of one dot and an additional fourth with the use of a second dot.

Normally, noteheads placed in spaces have the dot centered in the same space, while those placed on lines have the dot centered in the space directly above and to the right of the notehead, as in Example 3.9.

Example 3.9

Separately stemmed notes sharing a staff require relocation of placement for dots applied to those noteheads which have downward stems. Example 3.10 illustrates that while notes in upward stem positions are treated normally, those in downward stem positions which are placed on lines have dots centered in the lower adjacent space. Separately stemmed unison notes sharing a staff only require the use of one dot applicable to both notes, rather than two dots vertically aligned. (See Example 3.11.)

Example 3.10

Example 3.11

Inconsistent application

or

While unison notes of differing value placed in a space require performers to determine which of the notes is unaffected by the dot through note values which follow, the placement of the dot indicates which of the notes is undotted for those placed on a line, as shown in Example 3.12A. An acceptable alternative for dealing with dotted unisons of differing value on a shared staff consists of using two touching noteheads, the first of which is the undotted notehead.

Example 3.12A

Example 3.12B

Example 3.12C illustrates this alternate method. It is recommended that the alternate practice illustrated in Example 3.12B be reserved for use in rhythmically and metrically complex contexts where the use of the normal practice, as in Example 3.12A, may create ambiguity between the parts of a shared staff. (See Example 3.12C.)

Example 3.12C

Normal dotted unison practice

Alternate dotted unison practice

Example 3.13

Example 3.14

Augmentation dots applied to two or more noteheads forming intervals or chords without seconds are perpendicularly aligned and always centered in spaces, as in Example 3.13, and augmentation dots applied to individual intervals of a second are also perpendicularly aligned, as in Example 3.14. Note that the perpendicular alignment of dots applied to intervals of a second may require that a dot be placed more than a half staff-space away from its notehead.

Previously described dot placement practices should be adapted, whenever possible, to chords of three or more notes containing seconds. The myriad possibilities of notehead placement make formulation of inflexible rules impossible.

Augmentation dots may be applied to all rest symbols. Each rest symbol, as a single notational sign, only requires one dot which is always placed to the right of the rest symbol and centered in a staff-space. This practice is illustrated in Example 3.15.

Example 3.15

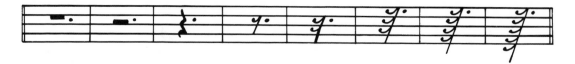

4
Beaming Practices

Example 4.1

Correct   Incorrect

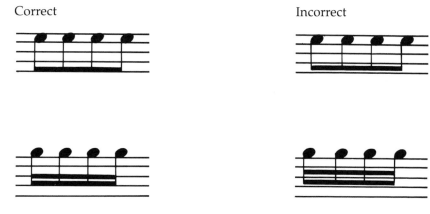

Example 4.2

- - - - - - - - - Implied leger line

Example 4.3

- - - - - - - Implied leger line

Beaming practices have been standardized and employed by reputable engraving firms for more than a century. Traditionally, all beams are of a thickness equal to half a staff-space. Two or more beams connecting a group of notes are spaced parallel. In manuscript notation, specifics of beam placement for one or more beams are based upon, but not identical to, those employed by engraving firms. Example 4.1 illustrates a basic notational principle applicable to both manuscript and engraved notation. Horizontal beams may not be placed in spaces without touching staff lines.

Single horizontal beams hang from a staff or implied leger line when attached to groups of notes whose noteheads are placed on spaces and have upward stems, as in Example 4.2. In Example 4.3, single horizontal beams sit on a staff or implied leger line when attached to groups of notes whose noteheads are placed on spaces and have downward stems. And, when applied to groups of notes whose noteheads are placed on lines and have upward or downward stems, single horizontal beams straddle a staff or implied leger line. (See Examples 4.4 and 4.5.)

Example 4.4

Example 4.5

Implied leger line

The placement of additional horizontal beams is governed by the position of a primary (single) beam. Primary beams which straddle lines require secondary beams to sit on or hang from an adjacent line when added to single-beamed groups of notes with downward or upward stems respectively. Secondary beams straddle adjacent lines when added to single-beamed groups of notes whose primary beams either hang or sit. Examples 4.6A and B illustrate the addition of secondary beams.

Example 4.6A

Implied leger line

Example 4.6B

Implied leger line

Implied leger line

Example 4.7

Implied leger lines

The addition of a third horizontal beam can create unequal spacing, which must be avoided. The repositioning of the primary beam, before the addition of the second and third beams, will eliminate this problem. Primary beams which hang or sit need not be repositioned and will allow the third beam to sit or hang respectively. Those which normally straddle require the stems to be extended to allow repositioning of the primary beam to a hang placement for upward-stemmed notes and a sit placement for downward-stemmed notes. Once the primary beam has been repositioned, the second beam is repositioned to the straddle placement and the third beam will sit for upward stems and hang for downward stems. Equal spacing will be maintained between all beams, as shown in Example 4.7.

Beam placement practices governing horizontal beams apply similarly to slant-beamed groups of notes. The complexities of slant beaming employed by engravers to maintain equal spacing between double and multiple beams and to avoid black and/or white wedges between beams and staff lines (which have a tendency to fill with ink during the reproduction process) may be generalized for use in manuscript notation. A basic generalization would be to restrict slant beaming to beamed groups of notes which consecutively ascend or descend in scale-like intervals, wide intervals and skips, and arpeggios. The angle of slant should be as small as possible and never more than one staff-space. Example 4.8 illustrates typical uses of slanting beams in manuscript notation, while Example 4.9 shows that beamed groups of notes whose noteheads have interrupted directional flow or are irregularly placed should be horizontally beamed.

Example 4.8

Implied leger lines

Example 4.9

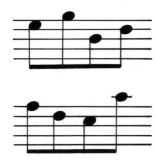

If a double beam requires a slant, neither beam may cross a staff line. In such instances, the crossing of staff lines may be avoided by decreasing the angle of slant or reverting to horizontal beaming, as in Example 4.10.

Example 4.10

Example 4.11

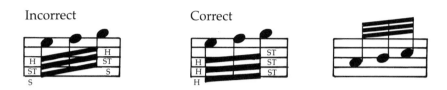

Incorrect   Correct

To avoid crossing staff lines in the placement of three or more beams, each of the beams must be repositioned to begin and end equally. This repositioning will increase the spacing between the beams uniformly and decrease the angle of slant. When all three beams are placed outside the staff, above or below, the repositioning of the beams is unnecessary. Example 4.11 illustrates these practices.

Example 4.12

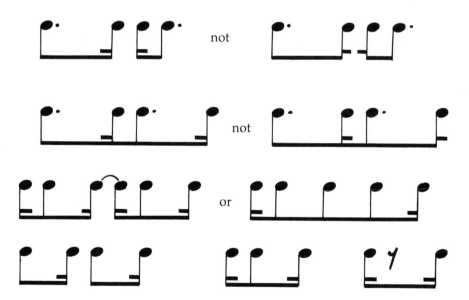

Individual notes of shorter value within a beamed group of notes are usually indicated by the fractional beam. All fractional beams are attached to stems and should be as long as the width of a notehead. Example 4.12 illustrates that fractional beams should be placed facing into the beats of which they are a part.

The proximity of horizontal or slant beams to noteheads of beamed groups of notes is governed by normal stem length. While any number of notes of a beamed group of notes may have stems lengthened to meet the outermost beam, no note may have a stem less than normal length. Normal stem lengths are indicated with an asterisk in Example 4.13.

Example 4.13

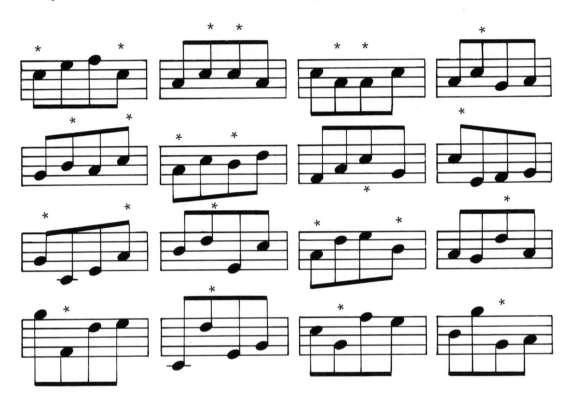

Example 4.14

in lieu of:

A beaming practice which is growing in popularity with composers and arrangers of rhythmically complex music consists of extending beam lengths to include rests that are integral parts of beamed groups of notes. Short stems, called stemlets, extend from the beam toward the rest but do not contact the rest. Example 4.14 illustrates beam extension and stemlet use.

5
Bar Lines and Repetition Signs

The five-line and time continuum line staves are intersected by perpendicular lines called bar lines. Bar lines on the five-line staff are drawn from the bottom to the top lines, while those drawn on the time continuum line staff intersect the line and are vertically equal to the percussion clef. Bar lines, as divisional symbols, may be of three distinct types, shown in Example 5.1. Type A is used to divide the staff into measures, while type C is used to designate the end of a musical work. Type B is used to indicate major sections of a musical work and to precede changes of key signature.

Example 5.1

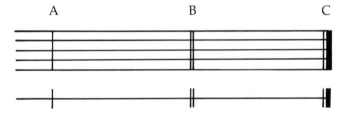

Type C and its vertical mirror image (‖), when combined with vertical dots, form sectional repeat signs. Sectional repeat signs may appear in the two practices illustrated in Examples 5.2A and B. In Example 5.2A, only the sectional repeat sign, whose dots are to the left of the bar lines, is required to return to the beginning of a work,

Example 5.2A

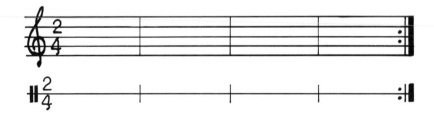

Example 5.2B

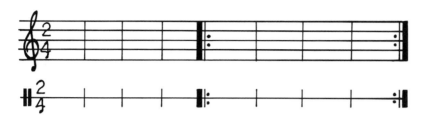

and Example 5.2B indicates that both the right and left dotted sectional repeat signs are required for any repeat within the body of a work.

Example 5.3A

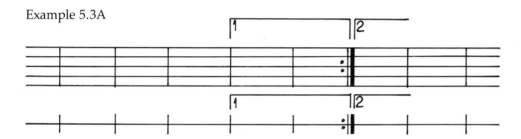

Example 5.3B

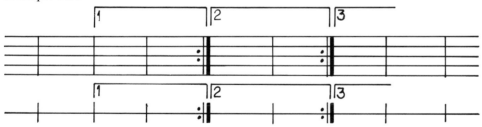

Example 5.3C

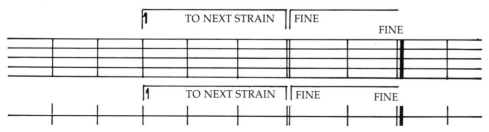

The left dotted sectional repeat sign may be used in combination with multiple endings. Measures of multiple endings must always be indicated with above-staff horizontal brackets. While the first bracket must span the entire length of nonrepeated measures, the final bracket need only span one complete measure, as illustrated in Examples 5.3A, B, and C. All horizontal brackets must be appropriately numbered or designated as to sequence of performance. The distance between the vertical legs of the brackets and the top line of the staff should be one staff-space, and the distance between the vertical legs of adjacent brackets is one staff-space and is aligned with the width of the thick bar of the sectional repeat or double bar line of Example 5.3C. All brackets, instructions, numbers, and related details should be positioned to avoid conflict with any notational symbols contained within the measures below the brackets. The final double bar line of Example 5.3C must be visually reinforced with the *fine* placed immediately above and before it.

The identical vertical alignment of equal numbers of measures from staff to staff on individual parts may create visual ambiguity for the performer and must be avoided. Offsetting the placement of bar lines on alternate staves will avoid this problem, as shown in Example 5.4.

Example 5.4

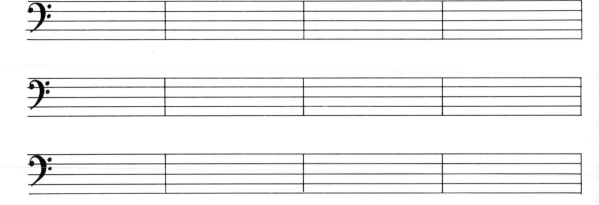

in lieu of:

Example 5.5A

Example 5.5B

The term *simile* (*sim.*) placed above a measure may be used to indicate the continuation of articulation signs or articulation patterns preceding it. Its placement must be preceded by one complete measure or pattern of the articulation to be continued. If a *simile* is to continue on a subsequent staff, a complete measure or pattern of the articulation must precede the placement of *simile* on that staff. Examples 5.5A and B illustrate the use of *simile*.

Repetition of individual measures may be indicated through the use of the dotted slant stroke. The slant stroke is placed between the second and fourth lines of the five-line staff and intersects the center line at mid-measure. A dot is centered in the third staff-space in vertical alignment with the lower left end of the stroke, while a second dot is centered in the second staff-space similarly aligned with the upper right end of the stroke. The dotted slant stroke may be placed mid-measure above, below, or centered on the time continuum line staff. If four or more measures employing the dotted slant stroke occur, a small, sequentially appropriate number in parentheses may be placed above every fourth measure as a counting aid for the performer. As with the use of the *simile* sign on subsequent staves, a dotted slant stroke measure must be preceded by one completely notated measure. Examples 5.6A, B, and C illustrate dotted slant stroke practice.

Example 5.6A

Example 5.6B

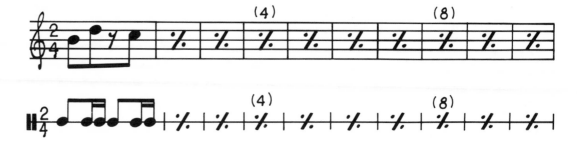

Example 5.6C

End of staff:

(4)

Subsequent staff

End of staff:

(4)

Subsequent staff

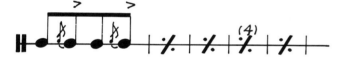

Example 5.7A

A pair of measures may be repeated through the use of the dotted slant double stroke. The double strokes are centered on a bar line, while the dots are placed as those illustrated in Example 5.6A. The practices illustrated in Examples 5.6B and C apply to the dotted slant double stroke, shown here in Examples 5.7A, B, and C.

Example 5.7B

Example 5.7C

End of staff:

Subsequent staff

End of staff:

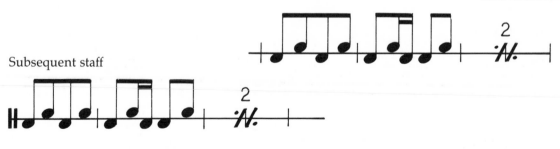

Subsequent staff

Example 5.8

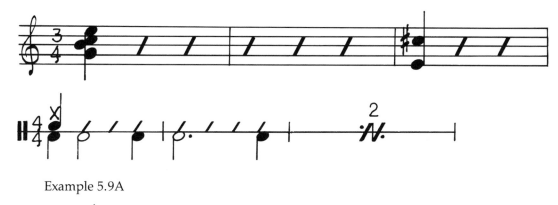

Example 5.9A

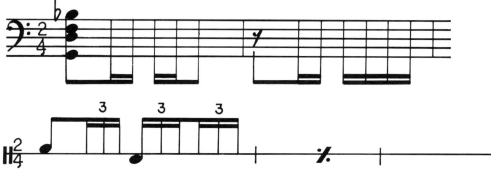

Successive repetitions of identical intervals or chords may be indicated with the use of the slant stroke (without dots) if the repetitions coincide with the prevailing beats. The slant stroke is placed between the second and fourth lines of the staff and intersects the center line. On the time continuum line staff, the slant stroke may be placed above, below, or centered on the line. All strokes must be spaced as if noteheads were present. Example 5.8 illustrates the use of the slant stroke.

Successive repetitions of identical intervals or chords which occur in rhythms may be indicated with headless stems after an initial notation of the interval or chord. While subsequent staves require the renotation of the interval or chord to precede the headless stems, renotation of an entire measure is unnecessary. Examples 5.9A and B illustrate this practice.

Example 5.9B

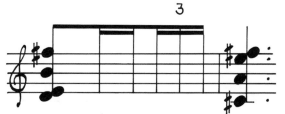

Dynamics and tempi indications are unaffected by the application of repetition signs, and may be included in the repetition or altered during the course of repetitions.

Larger sectional repetitions may be more practically indicated through the use of *Dal Segno*—(literally, to the sign (𝄋)—and various instructional phrases. The placement of instructional phrases is always above single staves or above familial stave systems in scores. Example 5.10 lists and defines the most commonly found traditional *Dal Segno* instructional phrases of sectional repetitions. The word *Segno* may or may not be present in the phrase.

Example 5.10

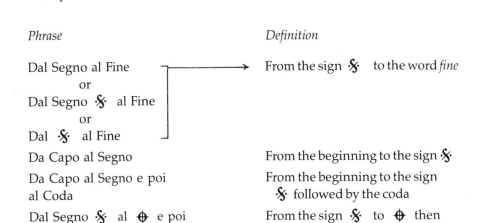

Phrase	Definition
Dal Segno al Fine	From the sign 𝄋 to the word *fine*
or	
Dal Segno 𝄋 al Fine	
or	
Dal 𝄋 al Fine	
Da Capo al Segno	From the beginning to the sign 𝄋
Da Capo al Segno e poi al Coda	From the beginning to the sign 𝄋 followed by the coda
Dal Segno 𝄋 al ⊕ e poi al Coda	From the sign 𝄋 to ⊕ then to the coda
Da Capo al Segno 𝄋 e poi al ⊕	From the beginning to the sign 𝄋 and then to ⊕
or	
Da Capo al 𝄋 e poi al ⊕	
Da Capo al Fine	From the beginning to *fine*

In all instances, the *Dal Segno* sign (𝄋) may be placed above the beginning or departure point of the section to be repeated, while the ⊕ sign is placed only above the point of departure, as shown in Example 5.11.

Example 5.11

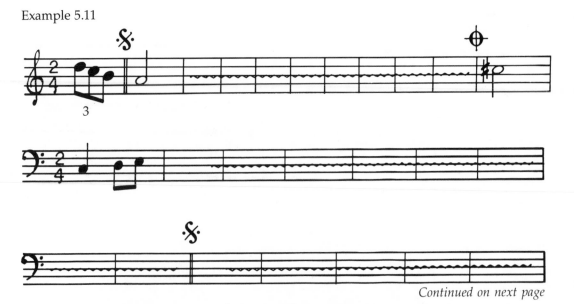

Continued on next page

Example 5.11 (*continued*)

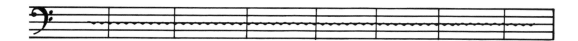

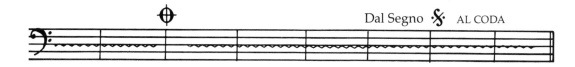

6
Ties and Slurs

The tie is an arced line which connects two successive notes of identical pitch. The tied notes become an unbroken sound equal in duration to the combined note values. While the tie may be horizontally arced above, within, or below the staff, the vertical distance of the arc should not be less than a third, nor more than a fourth, regardless of length. Generally, tied single notes have ties which arc away from stems or implied stems. Because tie ends should not touch noteheads and other attendant symbols, they should begin and end immediately after and before the midpoint of the quadrants of a notehead, as shown in Example 6.1A. Correct placement and arc of short and long ties are illustrated in Example 6.1B.

Example 6.1A

Beginning tie quadrant midpoints

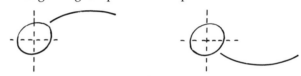

Ending tie quadrant midpoints

Example 6.1B

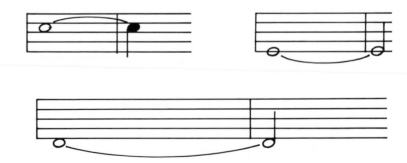

Example 6.2

Example 6.2 shows that tying practices may be applied to identical pitches that have been enharmonically spelled.

Example 6.3

Changes of stem direction of tied notes are reflected by a directional change of the tie arc. In such instances (Example 6.3), the tie will arc upward if one or both noteheads have a downward stem.

Example 6.4

End of staff

Subsequent staff

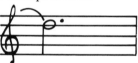

Ties which are interrupted at the end of a staff and are to be continued with the subsequent staff should arc in the direction of the second tied note. The arc of the tie should not touch or extend beyond the final bar line(s), including instances of simultaneous changes of key signature and/or time signatures. Further, the arc of an interrupted tie should not change direction with the subsequent staff application. Continuance of interrupted ties on subsequent staves begins immediately after the clef, key signature, or time signature, respectively. Example 6.4 illustrates these tying practices.

If a change of clef occurs at the end of a staff, simultaneously with an interrupted tie, the arc of the tie differs from normal practice in that it must arc immediately before the clef symbol (before the final bar line). Example 6.5 illustrates this alteration of interrupted tying practice.

Example 6.5

Ties which connect intervals of a second are always arced opposite one another, as in Example 6.6, and, similarly, ties of seconds occurring between voices sharing a staff are arced opposite one another regardless of reversed notehead placement, as in Example 6.7.

Example 6.6

Example 6.7

Ties of intervals or chords with an even number of noteheads and no seconds are arced opposite one another (Example 6.8A).

Example 6.8A

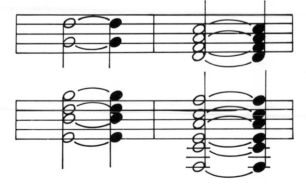

Example 6.8B

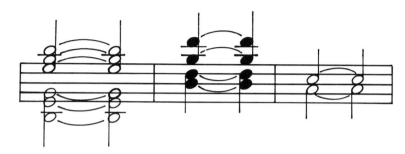

Ties of chords of two or more notes between voices sharing a staff are arced toward the stem or implied stem of each voice (Example 6.8B).

Example 6.9

The tie of the middle notehead within chords consisting of an odd number of noteheads and no seconds is governed by the placement of the notehead. The tie is arced upward if the middle notehead is on or above the center line of the staff, and downward if the middle notehead is placed below the center line. (See Example 6.9.)

Example 6.10

Ties of a second within chords of three or more notes are arced opposite one another, and determine the arc of all other ties above and/or below the second, as in Example 6.10.

Ties of two or more seconds within chords of four or more notes are tied as individual seconds with one exception: if the notehead placement of the seconds requires the internal tie arcs to overlap (Example 6.11), the internal ties must be arced in parallel with the external ties of the seconds.

Example 6.11

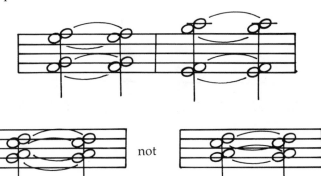

The slur is an arced line which begins and ends with the placement position accorded the staccato dot. It may be arced horizontally or obliquely below, through, or above the staff. Slurs indicate bowings for bowed stringed instruments, lack of articulation and/or legato playing for wind and keyboard instruments, and actual phrasing for definite pitch percussion instruments. Slurred passages consisting of all downward or upward stems have slurs above or below, respectively. Those with a mixture of upward and downward stems are always slurred above. Example 6.12 illustrates correct use of the slur.

Example 6.12

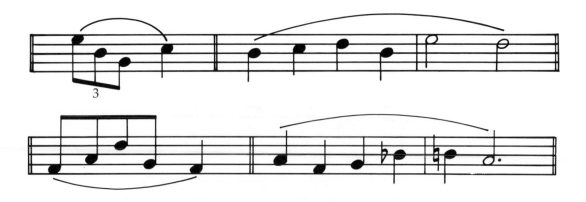

Example 6.13 illustrates that unstemmed notes are slurred as if stems were present.

Example 6.13

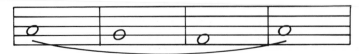

Example 6.14

Ties within slurred passages do not influence slurring practices, as shown in Example 6.14.

Example 6.15

Correct

Incorrect

Slurred passages which begin with tied notes (Example 6.15) require the slur to begin with the first of the tied notes, and slurred passages ending in tied notes (Example 6.16) require the slur to terminate with the final note.

Example 6.16

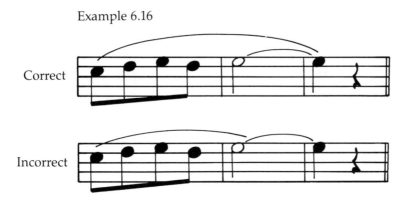

Correct

Incorrect

Slurs interrupted at the end of a staff do not arc downwardly or upwardly before stopping above or below the final bar line. Interruption and continuation of the slur are similar to those practices applicable to the tie. Example 6.17 illustrates arc placement of the slur at end of staff interruption and subsequent staff continuation.

Example 6.17

End of staff:

Subsequent staff

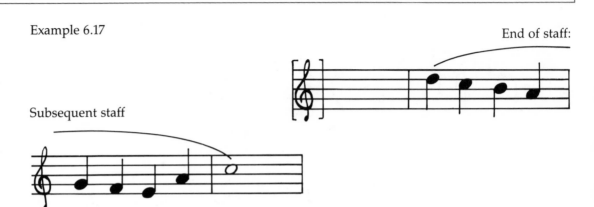

The slurring of two parts sharing a staff requires the slur to be both above and below the parts if any separate stemming is present, regardless of similarity of phrasing. Example 6.18 illustrates this practice.

Example 6.18

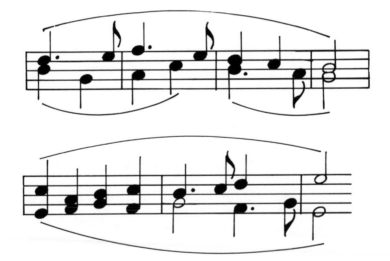

Example 6.19

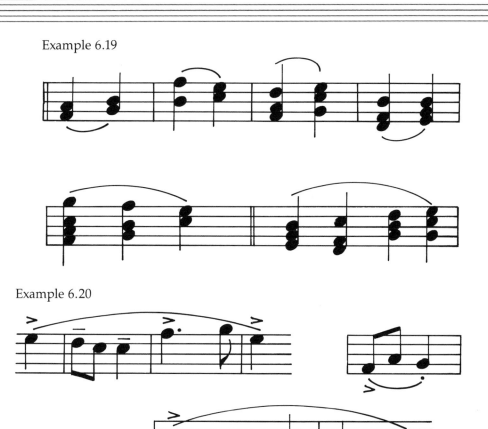

All practices governing the slur are applicable to the slurring of intervals or chords of two or more notes, as shown in Example 6.19.

Example 6.20

Generally, slurred (unbroken only) passages and intervals which begin and end with an accent require slur-ends to be placed between the note-head and the accent if one or both occur in the same placement position. All articulation signs applied to notes within a slurred passage are covered by the arc of the slur. These will be discussed further in Chapter 8, but Example 6.20 illustrates accents and articulation signs applied to slurred passages and intervals.

Example 6.21

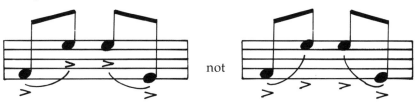

not

Passages or intervals consisting of widely separated notes whose nor-mally placed first and last accents would be too far from the noteheads to be visually effective, require the accents to be placed between the slurs and the noteheads, as shown in Example 6.21.

Unlike the placement of accents which begin and end slurred passages or intervals, staccato dots and tenuto lines in slurred passages and intervals are placed between the noteheads and the slur throughout the extent of the slur, a practice illustrated in Example 6.22.

Example 6.22

7
Accidentals and Key Signatures

In traditional notational practice alteration of pitch is designated by five symbols: sharp, flat, double sharp, double flat, and natural. Systemic groupings of sharps or flats form key signatures, while any of the alteration symbols employed individually and inconsistently are termed accidentals. Placement of all alteration symbols is always before the notehead to be altered.

The sharp, used to alter a pitch by raising it one semitone, consists of two vertically parallel lines that are intersected obliquely by two thicker parallel lines. The vertically parallel lines are two and one-half staff-spaces in length, one-half staff-space apart, and begin and end one-half staff-space apart, while the oblique parallel lines are each two staff-spaces in length, one-half staff-space apart, and begin and end vertically equal. The oblique lines should be slightly thickened to avoid being visually lost among staff lines. The placement of the sharp symbol on a line or space of the staff, as illustrated in Example 7.1, must be precise in that the parallelogram center of the symbol must either be intersected by a staff line or enclose a staff-space.

The flat, used to alter a pitch by lowering it one semitone, consists of a vertical line two and one-half staff-spaces in length with a half heart-like curvature attached to the lower right half of the line. Example 7.2 illustrates that the half heart-like curvature must either be intersected by a staff line or enclose a staff-space.

Key signatures which consist of one to seven sharps or flats, are formed as each sharp or flat is placed sequentially on specific lines and spaces of the staff. The traditional sharp or flat key signatures, correctly positioned with the G, F, C (alto), and C (tenor) clefs, are shown in Example 7.3.

The double sharp, used to raise a pitch by one whole step, may be described as the letter X, one staff-space in width and height, centered on a line or space of the staff, as in Example 7.4. Example 7.5 illustrates the double flat, which is used to lower a pitch by one whole step and consists of two flat symbols placed touching side by side.

Example 7.1

Example 7.2

Example 7.3

Example 7.4

Example 7.5

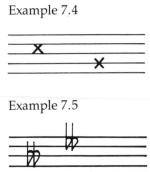

Example 7.6

The natural sign may be described as an incompletely formed sharp and is generally used to cancel any of the other alteration symbols. Like the oblique parallel lines of the sharp, those of the natural sign should be thickened for similar reasons but should not extend beyond the vertically parallel lines. (See Example 7.6.) Contrary to some incorrect common practices, the cancellation of a sharp, flat, double sharp, or double flat only requires a single natural sign, as shown in Example 7.7. Reduction of a double sharp or double flat to a single sharp or flat, respectively, only requires the appropriate single accidental (Example 7.8).

Example 7.7

Correct

Incorrect

Example 7.8

Correct

Incorrect

Generally, an accidental only alters the specific pitch to which it has been applied and does not alter similarly named pitches of other octaves, in other clefs, or on other staves. Further, the accidental remains in effect on that specific pitch for the entire measure or until it is altered by another accidental. It is common to find accidentals used as reminders in complex or ambiguous passages and after changes of key signature. These are termed courtesy accidentals and aid the performer. Example 7.9A illustrates that, although octaves sharing like letter names are not altered by an accidental, it is advisable to include courtesy accidentals for purposes of clarity and accuracy; their correct common uses are shown in Example 7.9B. It should be noted that extensive use of courtesy accidentals in either scores or individual parts may become a counterproductive distraction.

Example 7.9A

Courtesy accidentals

Example 7.9B

Example 7.10

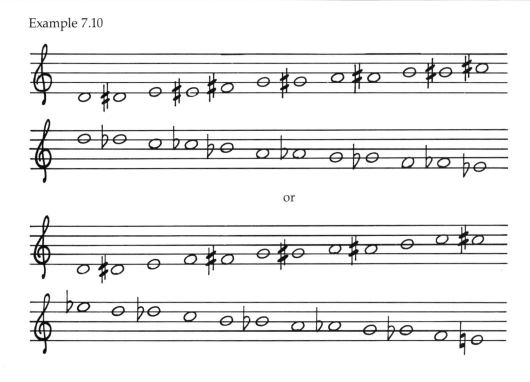

or

As shown in Example 7.10, in traditional notational practice the use of accidentals in chromatic scales is governed by two general practices that are relatively unaffected by prevailing key signatures: Ascending chromatic scales should employ sharps, and descending chromatic scales should employ flats.

Example 7.11A

Required accidentals

not

Examples 7.11A and B illustrate that accidentals altering pitches of parts sharing a staff are mutually exclusive, while those altering pitches among passages of intervals and chords on a single stem are not.

Example 7.11B

Courtesy accidentals

Ascending and descending passages depicted in Example 7.12, may require the repetition of key signature sharps or flats as courtesy accidentals to avoid ambiguity.

Example 7.12

An altered pitch which occurs before and after a change of clef requires the reiteration of the accidental after the new clef, as shown in Example 7.13.

Example 7.13

Required

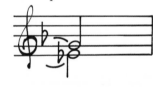

Accidentals which apply to tied notes (Example 7.14) may be reiterated on the subsequent staff if the tie is continued from the previous staff.

Example 7.14

Subsequent staff

Accidentals which apply to notes tied across a bar line in the course of a staff are not reiterated after the barline (before the end of the tie). Example 7.15 illustrates that the accidental must be reiterated if the previously altered pitch is to be repeated in the new measure.

Example 7.15

Example 7.16

Courtesy accidentals

If the altered pitch is repeated within the same measure, accidentals should not normally be reiterated. However, accidentals should be reiterated if, after the initial appearance, the complexities of intervening notes would give reason to doubt the identity of the originally altered pitch. A passage which requires the courtesy repetition of previously used accidentals is shown in Example 7.16.

Example 7.17

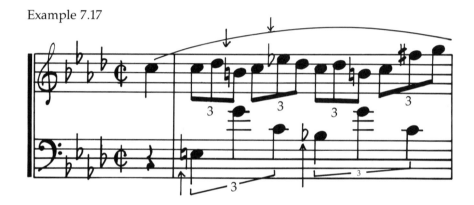

An altered pitch on one staff of a multiple-stave system requires the use of courtesy accidentals for all similarly named pitches which may be present on other staves in the same subsequent measures (Example 7.17).

Example 7.18

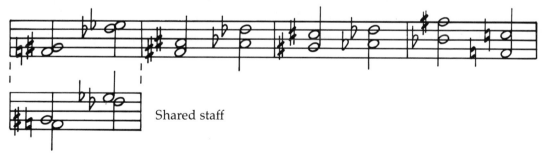

Shared staff

Accidentals applied to both notes of vertical two-note intervals, consisting of seconds through fifths, are placed diagonally left from the top pitch to the bottom pitch. Accidentals applied to seconds of a shared staff are placed diagonally left and upward from the bottom pitch to the top pitch, to reflect the change in notehead placement. As with the use of a single accidental, the accidental nearest the noteheads or stem should be at a distance of one staff-space. These practices are illustrated in Example 7.18.

Accidentals applied to both pitches of a vertical interval of a sixth are placed similarly to those illustrated in Example 7.18 with one exception: if the upper note of the sixth is altered with a flat, the accidentals are perpendicularly aligned because the flat symbol will not physically contact the accidental immediately below. Example 7.19 illustrates the placement of two accidentals applied to pitches of the interval of a sixth.

Example 7.19

Accidentals applied to both notes of vertical intervals of sevenths or more are always perpendicularly aligned (Example 7.20).

Example 7.20

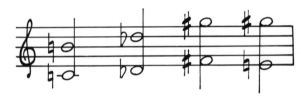

Three-note chord combinations without seconds, involving three accidentals, require the center accidental to be placed left of the bottom (second from the right) accidental if the interval between the upper and lower pitches is less than a sixth. If the top and bottom pitches form the interval of a sixth and the top pitch is altered by a flat, the top and bottom accidentals are perpendicularly aligned, while the center accidental is placed left of the alignment, as in Example 7.21.

Example 7.21

Example 7.22

Three-note chord combinations without seconds, involving three accidentals, whose outer pitches are at the interval of a seventh or more from the center pitch, require all accidentals to be vertically aligned. If either outer pitch is less than a seventh from the center pitch, outer accidentals are vertically aligned, and the center accidental is placed immediately left of the alignment. Example 7.22 illustrates these practices.

Example 7.23A

Example 7.23B

Three-note chords involving three accidentals and in downward stem position, consisting of a note placed below a second at intervals of a third through that of a fifth from the top pitch, have accidentals placed right to left (top notehead, bottom notehead, center notehead). Those in upward stem position, consisting of a note placed above a second at intervals of a third through that of a fifth from the bottom pitch, have accidentals placed right to left in the following sequence: center notehead, top notehead, and bottom notehead. These practices are shown in Examples 7.23A and B.

Three-note chords involving three accidentals and in downward or upward stem position, consisting of a note placed below a second at a distance of a sixth from a top pitch which has been altered by a sharp or natural, have accidentals placed similarly to those shown in Example 7.23A, and are illustrated in Example 7.24.

Example 7.24

Three-note chords involving three accidentals and in downward stem position, consisting of a note placed above a second at intervals of a fourth through that of a sixth from the bottom pitch (Example 7.25), have accidentals placed right to left in the following sequence: top notehead, center notehead, and bottom notehead.

Example 7.25

Three-note chords involving three accidentals and in downward or upward stem position, consisting of a note placed above or below a second at intervals of a seventh or more, or of a sixth from a pitch which has been altered by a flat, have accidentals placed right to left in the following sequence: top and bottom accidentals vertically aligned with the center accidental left of the alignment, as shown in Example 7.26.

Example 7.26

Example 7.27

Chord combinations involving the use of four or more accidentals are too varied in number to formulate inflexible rules governing sequential placement of accidentals. As a general practice, the top and bottom accidentals should be vertically aligned when possible, while internal accidentals may be placed left of the alignment from the next uppermost notehead diagonally left in a downwardly direction. Example 7.27 illustrates the suggested placement of four or more accidentals applied to chord combinations of four or more noteheads.

Example 7.28

End of staff:

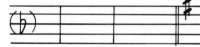

Subsequent staff

The key signature is always placed at the beginning of each staff immediately following the clef. The first sharp or flat of the signature should be no less than one staff-space from the clef. Key signature changes may occur at any point in the course of a staff and, with one exception, must be preceded by a double bar line. Changes of key signature which occur at the beginning of a staff are immediately preceded by a double bar line but are preceded by the notation of the change at the end of the previous staff. Because this cautionary placement of the key signature change is preceded by a bar line, the staff line is left open. The notation of key signature changes is illustrated in Example 7.28.

Key signature changes do not require either repeating the clef sign (unless the clef is also changed at that precise point) or the cancellation of the previous key signature, except before the notation of the new key signature. If the prevailing key signature involves the use of one or more sharps or flats and is followed by the the C major or A minor key signature, it must be cancelled after a double bar line by appropriately placed natural signs, as in Examples 7.29 and 7.29A.

Example 7.29

Example 7.29A

End of staff:

Subsequent staff

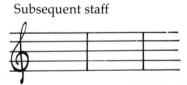

Example 7.30

Example 7.30 illustrates commonly found errors at key signature changes.

End of staff:

8
Articulation and Miscellaneous Signs

Articulation signs may be placed above and/or below noteheads or stems individually, in combinations, or with slurs and ties. Example 8.1 lists and illustrates seven basic, universally understood and employed articulation signs.

Example 8.1

Name	Sign	Size particulars (if applicable)
Normal staccato		
Staccatissimo		Height of notehead; widest point: half notehead width
Normal accent		Width of notehead
Strong accent		Height of notehead; width of notehead
Weak beat		Height of notehead; width of notehead
Strong beat		Approximately a 45° angle; similar to staccatissimo
Tenuto		Width of notehead

Example 8.2

Articulation signs which are consistently placed outside the staff are the weak beat (∨), strong beat (◢), staccatissimo (▼), and strong accent (∧). Example 8.2 illustrates that individual placement of these articulation signs may not be less than the distance of a third above or below noteheads. Alternate placement positions (in parentheses) for the signs may be used when crowded conditions will not permit normal placement.

The normal accent sign (>) is usually placed outside the staff above or below noteheads or stems, but may be placed within the staff when placement outside the staff would prove impractical or less effectual. In such cases, the placement should be centered in a staff-space a fourth from a notehead placed on a line or a fifth from a notehead placed in a space. Normal accents placed within the staff at stem-ends, such as those employed for separately stemmed notes, are centered in a staff-space a minimum of a third from the stem-end. Example 8.3 illustrates placement of normal accent signs above, below, and within the staff.

Example 8.3

Example 8.4

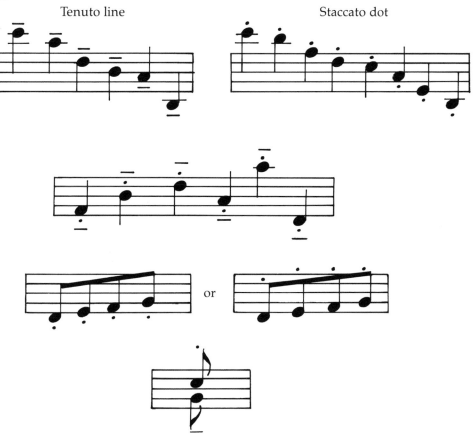

Tenuto line   Staccato dot

or

When individually employed, the tenuto (–) and staccato (•) signs are placed above or below noteheads or at stem-ends, inside or outside the staff. Inside the staff, they should be centered in a space and never placed on a line. Both are placed one staff-space from noteheads on spaces and one-and-a-half spaces away from noteheads on lines. When employed together, the staccato dot is placed as previously described, while the tenuto line is placed an additional staff-space beyond the staccato. Placement of both the staccato dot and tenuto line at stem-ends, individually or in combination, is similar to their notehead placement in that each is centered above the notehead and at a third or fourth beyond the stem-end. Example 8.4 illustrates individual and combined placement of the staccato dot and tenuto line, and Example 8.4A shows that the placement of appropriate articulation signs above and below whole notes is governed by the implied presence of stems.

Example 8.4A

In traditional notational practice all dynamics symbols and abbreviations are placed below the staff for instrumental music, and above for vocal music. Instrumental music scores and individual parts require dynamics to be specifically placed directly below the first note affected, while such dynamics in vocal scores and parts are similarly placed above the staff. Dynamics are rarely placed within the body of the staff or touching any of its lines. (See Example 8.5.)

Example 8.5

Instrumental

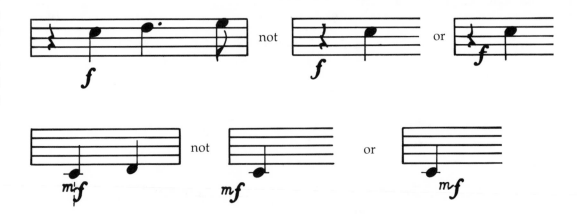

Continued on next page

Example 8.5 (*continued*)

Dynamics symbols such as those illustrated in Example 8.5 are symmetrically placed as near the affected passages as notational considerations and space will allow. In rare instances they may be placed with slightly oblique angles, as shown in Example 8.6.

Example 8.6

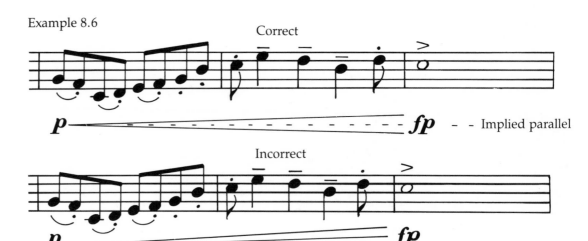

Beyond the basic practices illustrated by Examples 8.5 and 8.6 above, myriad possibilities of dynamics application render inflexible rules impractical. Example 8.7 lists general guidelines governing the use and placement of dynamics.

The placement of three or more polyphonic voices on a single staff is impractical and should be avoided.

Example 8.7

Instrumental Music

Staff System	Placement
Single staves on scores and parts	Below the staff
Single staves shared and separately stemmed	Stem-ends
Multiple staves such as employed for piano	Between staves is preferred but crowded inter-stave space will allow above and below stave placement
Multiple staves such as employed for organ	Between the manual staves and similar to piano for crowded space Below the pedal staff
Full scores such as employed for band, wind ensemble, and orchestral ensembles	Similar to single staves above

Vocal/Choral Music

Staff System	Placement
Single and shared staves including separate stemming	Above staves (because all texts are placed below staves)
Two stave reductions	Above or below with text between
Piano accompaniment	Similar to piano above

Example 8.8A

Required tempo

MODERATO ♩ = 120

Suggestive tempo

MODERATO (♩ = c.120)

Example 8.8B

♩ = 120

←♩=♩·→

Primary tempo indications, such as *allegro, andante,* and *moderato,* should be appropriately capitalized and placed above the staff for both instrumental and vocal music. Orchestral scores require the primary tempo indication to be placed above the wind/percussion and string systems of the score page, while similar placement in band and wind ensemble scores is above the woodwind and brass systems. The primary tempo indication placement for vocal/choral scores is above the voice system and above the accompaniment (keyboard) system. Metronomic indications may be placed immediately following the primary tempo indication and need not be enclosed in parentheses unless such indications are suggestive rather than required. Example 8.8A illustrates metronomic indications which are applicable to primary tempo indications, and Example 8.8B illustrates those which may be applied to tempo changes between major sections.

Tempo alteration instructions, such as *ritardando* (*rit.* or *ritard.*), *accelerando* (*accel.*), *rallentando* (*rall.* or *rallen.*), and others, should be placed above staves for all genre. Frequently, as is the case with instrumental and vocal scores, the lack of notational space between individual staves requires that tempo alteration instructions be placed systemically by familial group. As with normal placement between staves for keyboard music, crowded inter-stave space permits placement of tempo alteration instructions above the upper staff.

Performance instructions, such as *sempre, subito (sub.), marcato (marc.)*, and so on, are dynamically related and similarly placed. Expressive instructions, such as *affettuoso* and *leggiero,* and technical instructions, such as *pizzicato (pizz.), arco, divisi (div.), solo, soli,* muting, instrument changes, and others are not dynamically related and are preferably placed above staves.

The fermata sign (⌒) is used to sustain sound and silence beyond the prevailing value of the symbol to which it is applied. Except for use with separately stemmed parts sharing a staff, it is always placed above the staff, and never within or touching the staff. The ends of the arc portion should be approximately the width of a leger line with an arc of a third. The dot is centered between the arc-ends and a third above the staff or any of the following which may be above the staff: noteheads, stem-ends, tie and slur-ends, and articulation signs. During the course of a slur, the fermata should be placed below the arc of the slur. Example 8.9A illustrates correct placement of the fermata in a variety of uses, and Example 8.9B shows that fermatas may be applied upside down below the staff when applied to separately stemmed parts sharing a staff.

Example 8.9A

Example 8.9B

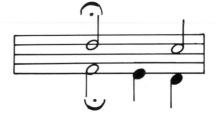

Example 8.10

The comma (**,**) and caesura (⫽) refer to silence and may be used to interrupt sound and/or measured flow of time. The comma is normally placed above the staff, while the caesura normally intersects the top two lines of the staff, as shown in Example 8.10.

Example 8.11

Single staves

Shared staves

Grace notes are always notated half normal size and, with the exception of a shared staff, with upward stems regardless of position relative to the staff. Single grace notes are notated as eighth notes, while those with two consecutive noteheads and three or more noteheads, are notated as beamed sixteenth and thirty-second notes respectively. Single grace notes have an upward diagonal slash through the stem and flag. The beamed grace notes have a similar slash intersecting the left corner of the juncture of beam and stem.

Grace notes occurring on parts of a shared staff are stemmed in the same direction as the part to which they apply. Example 8.11 illustrates single, double, and multiple grace notes on single and shared staves.

Notes used for cues in instrumental parts are always half the size of the prevailing notation. Cues which lie primarily above the center line of the staff have upward stems exclusively, while those below the center line have downward stems exclusively. All cues must be notated at the concert or transposed pitch level of the instrument in whose parts they appear. Indefinite pitch percussion cues should be notated without pitch implication and placed above the staff. Example 8.12 illustrates notation of pitched and indefinite pitch cues.

In normal practice, trills are notated by placing the abbreviation *tr* directly above the primary note (head or stem-end) upon which the trill is based. The trill sign should be followed by a tightly waved line if the trill is to span more than one beat in the prevailing time signature. Trilled one-beat notes do not require the use of the wavy line unless followed by a rest. In such cases, and those lasting more than one beat, the wavy line must extend to the completion of the trill, with a short vertical stroke downward at the precise point of termination, whether rest, note, or bar line. Example 8.13 illustrates the use of the trill sign singly and in combination with the wavy line.

Example 8.12

Pitched

Indefinite Pitch

Example 8.13

Example 8.14

Legato slurring of consecutive single note trills may be indicated by the placement of one trill sign above the first trilled note and a wavy line extending from that point over all other single notes to be trilled. The wavy line must have the short downward stroke at the point of termination. Example 8.14 illustrates this practice.

Example 8.15

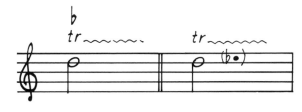

Traditionally, it is understood that the primary note is the lowest pitch of the two notes to be trilled. Unless otherwise indicated, the upper note of the trill will either be diatonically dictated by the prevailing key signature or, in the absence of a key signature, trilled as if the key of C major prevails. Altered upper notes may be indicated by placing an appropriate accidental above the trill abbreviation, or a black and unstemmed cue-sized notehead designating the altered pitch in parentheses immediately after the primary note as in Example 8.15.

Example 8.16

The upper note of a trill, notated as a grace note, may precede the primary note if the trill is to begin on that pitch (Example 8.16), or, if a trill begins with two or more opening pitches, those pitches may be notated as multiple grace notes preceding the primary note (Example 8.17).

Example 8.17

Cue-sized notes may be used to end a trill followed by a rest, or to lead a trill to a subsequent note. If the trill is followed by a rest, the cue-sized notes should be slurred from the primary note, while cue-sized notes ending a trill and leading to a subsequent note should be slurred to that note. Example 8.18 illustrates these practices.

Example 8.18

Tremolos may be placed in two basic classifications: a note, interval, or chord in measured or unmeasured repetition; and trill tremolos consisting of measured or unmeasured alternation of two pitches more than a whole step apart.

If the repetitions of a note, interval, or chord are measured, those repetitions may be represented notationally through the use of oblique beams placed through the stem or implied stem. The length of the oblique beams, a half staff-space apart, are the width of a notehead, are angled upward regardless of stem direction or beam placement, and are centered between the notehead and the end of a stem. Three or more oblique beams require unbeamed stems to be lengthened, while two or more oblique beams require beamed stems to be lengthened. While the note symbol indicates the total duration of the tremolo, the number of oblique beams, which are accumulative, indicate the individual note values of the repetitions, as in Example 8.19.

Example 8.19

Continued on next page

Example 8.19 (*continued*)

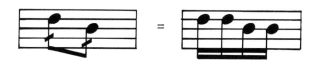

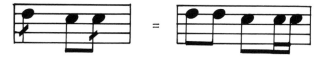

Example 8.20

Broken ties are used to connect continuous tremolos within a measure or across a bar line (Example 8.20). All previously discussed practices governing tied notes are applicable to broken-tied tremolos.

Example 8.21

VIVACE
Trem.

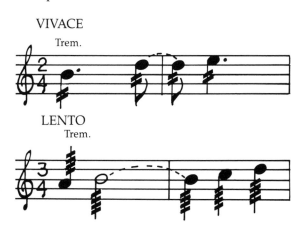

LENTO
Trem.

The practices governing measured tremolos may be applied to unmeasured tremolos. The use of two oblique beams in fast tempi indicates rapid tremolos, while as many as four oblique beams in slow tempi indicate rapid tremolos. (See Example 8.21.)

The trill tremolo is indicated through seemingly anomalous notation because the note symbol indicating the total duration of the tremolo is given twice with two tremolo oblique beams placed between them. For example, two whole notes with two oblique tremolo beams centered between them indicate that the tremolo is equal in duration to one of the whole notes, while two quarter notes with two oblique tremolo beams between them indicate that the tremolo is equal in duration to one of the quarter notes. Half-note trill tremolos are treated somewhat differently in that the two half notes (or dotted half notes) may be connected by a single beam with the two oblique tremolo beams placed between that beam and the noteheads. The single beam does not alter the basic value of the half notes. While whole notes, as previously stated, have two oblique tremolo beams centered between the noteheads, quarter notes and all beamed notes are notated normally—that is, quarter notes are not connected by a beam, eighth notes have one connecting beam, sixteenth notes have two connecting beams, and so on — and they have two oblique tremolo beams placed between the stem-ends or connecting beams and the noteheads. Example 8.22 illustrates trill tremolo practice.

Example 8.22

Total duration

Appendix

ENGRAVING AND PUBLISHING FIRMS

Alfred Lengnick & Company, Ltd.
Alphonse Leduc & Cie
American Institute of Musicology
    (Hänssler-Verlag, Neuhausen-Stuttgart)
Anglo-Soviet Music Press, Ltd., London
A-R-Editions
Arthur F. Schmidt Publishing Co.
Associated Music Publishers
Bärenreiter-Verlag, Kassel
Boosey & Hawkes, Inc., New York
Breitkopf & Härtel in Leipzig
Broude Brothers, Music Publishers
Carl Fisher, Inc., New York
Casa Editrice Paideia di Brescia
Charles B. Hansen Music Publications
Charles Foley, New York
Concordia Publishing House,
    St. Louis, MO
Doblinger and Universal Edition, Wein
Durand et Cie. (Paris)
Editio Musica, Budapest
Edition Peters
Editions Max Eschig (Paris)
Edward B. Marks Music Corporation
Elkan-Vogel Co., Inc.
Faber Music Limited (London)
Flores Musicales Belgicae
Foetisch Freres S. A., Ediyeurs,
    Lausanne (Paris)
Galaxy Music Publications
G. Schirmer, Inc.
Harvard University Press
Heugel et Cie. (Paris)

Hinrichsen Edition Ltd., Bach House
Instytut Fryderyka Chopina (National
    Printing Works), Warsaw, Poland
International Music Co., New York
Jenson Music, Inc.
Kalmus Music Publishing
Ludwig Music Publishing Company
Merion Music, Inc.
Musica Sacra et Profana (Berkeley, CA)
New Music Edition Corporation Publisher
Northridge Music Company
Prostat Apud G. Alsbach & Co.,
    (Amsterdam)
Russian publications (National Printing
    Works), Moscow, USSR
S. A. Edizioni Suvini Zerboni — Milano
Schott & Co., Ltd.
Shattinger International Music Corp.,
    New York
Stainer & Bell, Ltd.
Swets & Zeitlinger N. V. (Amsterdam)
Willy Muller, Suddeitscher Musikverlag,
    Heidelberg
Zenemukiado Vallalat, Budapest

Bibliography

Ahlstrom, David. "The Notation Trap: Do Symbols Rule the Composer?" *Music Educators Journal* 57 (May 1957): 46–47.

Bartolozzi, Bruno. "Proposals for Changes in Musical Notation." Trans. by Brooks Shepard. *Journal of Music Theory* 5, no. 2 (1961): 297–301.

Benward, Bruce. *Music in Theory and Practice*, 2 vols. Iowa: Wm. C. Brown Company Publishers, 1982.

Boehm, Laszlo. *Modern Music Notation*. New York: G. Schirmer, 1961.

Brown, Earle. "Notational Problems." *American Society of University Composers: Proceedings* 5 (1970): 8–14.

Bussler, Ludwig. *Elements of Notation and Harmony*. New York: G. Schirmer, 1907.

Cope, David. *New Music Notation*. Dubuque: Kendal/Hunt, 1976.

Donato, Anthony. *Preparing Music Manuscripts*. Englewood Cliffs, N.J.: Prentice-Hall, Inc., 1963.

Forte, Allen. *Tonal Harmony in Concept and Practice*. New York: Holt, Rinehart, and Winston, Inc., 1974.

Gray, Norman. *A Note on Music Engraving and Printing*. London: Boosey & Hawkes, Inc., 1952.

Groves Dictionary of Music and Musicians, "Notation." London: Macmillan Ltd., 1980.

Hauser, Arlin C. *Modern Music Notation*. La Crescenta: Melograf Music Association, 1948.

Hindemith, Paul. *Elementary Training for Musicians*. New York: Associated Music Publishers, 1949.

Lester, Joel. *Harmony in Tonal Music*. 2 vols. New York: A. Knopf, Inc., 1982.

McHose, Allen I. *The Contrapuntal Harmonic Technique of the 18th Century*. New York: Appleton-Century-Crofts, Inc., 1947.

Murphy, H. A., and E. J. Stringham. *Creative Harmony and Musicianship*. Englewood Cliffs, N.J.: Prentice-Hall, Inc., 1951.

O'Brien, James. "Teach the Principles of Notation, Not Just the Symbols." *Music Educators Journal*, no. 9 (May 1974): 38–42.

Osburn, Leslie. "Notation Should Be Metric and Representational." *Journal of Research in Music Education* 14, no. 2 (1966): 67–83.

Ottman, Richard. *Elementary Harmony*. Englewood Cliffs, N.J.: Prentice-Hall, Inc., 1961.

Perkins, John McIvor. "Note Values." *Perspectives of New Music* 3, no. 2 (1965): 47–57.

Piston, W., and Mark DeVoto. *Harmony*. 4th ed. New York: W. W. Norton & Company, Inc., 1978.

Pooler, Frank, and Brent Pierce. *New Choral Notation*. 2d ed. New York: Walton Music, 1973.

Read, Gardner. *Music Notation: A Manual of Modern Practice*. 2d ed. Boston: Allyn & Bacon, 1969.

———. *Modern Rhythmic Notation*. Bloomington: Indiana Univ. Press, 1978.

Roemer, Clinton. *The Art of Music Copying*. Sherman Oaks: Roerick Music, 1973.

Rosenthal, Carl. *Practical Guide to Music Notation*. New York: MCA Music, 1967.

Ross, Ted. *The Art of Music Engraving and Processing*. Rev. ed. New York: Hansen Books, 1970.

Sessions, Roger. *Harmonic Practice*. Boston: Harcourt, Brace & Company, 1951.

Stone, Kurt. "Problems and Methods of Notation." *Perspectives of New Music* 1, no. 2 (1963): 9–13.

———. *Music Notation in the Twentieth Century*. New York: W. W. Norton & Company, Inc., 1980.

———. "Symposium on New Music Notation." *Contemporary Music Newsletter* 7, no. 1 (January 1973): 1–2.

Tischler, R. *Practical Harmony*. Boston: Allyn & Bacon, Inc., 1964.

Warfield, Gerald. *How to Write Music Manuscript in Pencil*. New York: David McKay Company, Inc., 1977.

Williams, Ken. *Music Preparation: A Guide to Music Copying*. New York: Ken J. Williams Publications, 1980.

Index